JOYS AND SORROWS OF ADOPTION

Joys and Sorrows of Adoption

An Inspirational Book About Love, Understanding, and Engagement

GRACIELA CONGOTE KEANE

Joys and Sorrows of Adoption
By Graciela Congote Keane

Edited by Paula Schonewald

© 2020 by Graciela Congote Keane

Printed in the United States of America

ISBN: 9798676856571

Book design by Valley House Books
Cover design by Rob Buscher

Contents

ACKNOWLEDGMENTS AND CONTRIBUTIONS

MY IMMENSE GRATITUDE goes first of all to my husband John and our two sons, Edward and Robert, who believed I could and should write this book. We all knew there were going to be moments of reckoning but felt we would be stronger and become closer because of it. The book is a "mea culpa" under disguise; they know what I mean...

To my editor, Paula Schonewald, who has read and re-read the manuscript, spent time thinking for me, held my hand and lifted my spirits when things got stuck. Many thanks, Paula.

My early readers: how I love you and feel grateful for your generosity and courage. Reading a book draft is not exactly a fun activity but you came through with flying colors, providing useful and heart-felt ideas which enriched the book.

My deepest gratitude to all of them: Erika Ridgeway, Sheila and Jim Mack, Albie Williams, Joan Fraser, Martha Netherton, Steve Coles, Deborah P., Edward Keane, John Keane, Robert Keane and Angela Barnes.

I want to express my gratitude to Nancy Newton Verrier whose book *The Primal Wound* inspired me to tackle the adoption issues which plague so many adoptees and parents. Nancy's book, now translated into 4 languages, opens a door that invites adoptees and adoptive parents to look into themselves and emotionally move to a better place in life. Thank you, Nancy.

The book would still be resting in a drawer if the joint efforts of Erika and Glenn had not led me to Jim Watson of Valley House Books in Vermont, who told me yes, the book could be printed on time to meet my deadlines. He has demonstrated a great "can do" attitude, service spirit and commitment. I will be forever grateful to you, Jim.

I OWE THE inspiration to write this book to our sons, now 36 and 37 years old, whose courage and resilience have helped us overcome the difficult moments in our life together as well as to enjoy the many happy ones. Our sons' powerful testimonials and expressed feelings are precious windows into the life of an adoptee. We admire their generosity in accepting and forgiving us for the mistakes we unintentionally made in raising them. My husband and I feel grateful to have them in our lives.

INTRODUCTION

Meeting Our Infant Children

WE ARRIVED AT the given address and found an old building in need of painting and a good cleaning. We climbed a flight of stairs and found ourselves in a large room with five cribs in its center. The place was dark and gloomy. The only light came from two windows at the far end of the room. There was no heat on a cold, mid-April day in the city of Buenos Aires. We stood at the threshold for a moment, and heard a voice saying: "Yours is the one in the first crib; you can dress him on the table behind you." We approached the crib and saw a two week old baby, still in a fetal position, with legs and arms curled towards the body and fists tightly closed; he wore a skimpy outfit and had no pillow or blanket. We said, "Hi, Baby, we have come for you." Hearing us, he slowly turned his head, fixed his eyes on us and stared at us, a pronounced frown on his little face. Sorrow overcame me seeing such a sad, anguished expression on someone so young. We brought him to the table, and dressed him warmly while talking gently to him. The caretaker then said: "He does not sleep very much, eats very little and does not cry much."

Once in the car I put him in an infant sleeping bag and put his head right over my heart. To my surprise, he fell asleep within moments. Because of my training in Psychology and Early Childhood Special Education and several years of work with young children I was expecting him to struggle in my arms. However, this child who apparently had lacked human contact and had suffered physical and emotional stress for the first two weeks of his life seemed to welcome my arms around him. I concluded he was exhausted and was reacting to a friendlier physical environment and perhaps the beating of my heart. A flood of relief went through me while I rocked him during the trip home.

Seventeen months after receiving our first son my husband and I decided to apply for a second child. We called our social worker on a Friday morning expressing our wishes. She said she would call us later. Four hours later she called and gave us the address of a judicial office and told us to be there at 9am the next Monday. We thought, here goes the first interview of the lot…

On Monday morning, my husband and I, together with our seventeen month old son, Miguel Angel, (now Robert Andrew) arrived at the judge's office as instructed. The judge invited us to sit. We asked our son to sit on the floor and gave him a book. The judge looked at us, looked at our child who was sitting with ramrod straight posture on the floor and said, "Does that child know how to read?" We looked at our son and saw that he was looking at the book, moving his head and lips, as if reading, but was holding the book upside down…! We explained to his Honor that no, he was just pretending to read. He then proceeded to write on a piece of paper, gave it to us and explained: "Be at this address at 9am Thursday morning. Go to the maternity ward to pick up a newborn baby boy." We went home realizing we had become instant parents of a second child…No interviews, no months of waiting…We felt a mixture of excitement and concern; we only had THREE days to prepare for our second son's arrival…!

At the hospital, a guide took us to the maternity ward; we were greeted by a nurse standing next to a table with a newborn baby on it. Asleep, he looked peaceful, rosy-cheeked and well-fed. He was dressed with simple but clean clothing and wrapped in a warm blanket. The nurse explained that she had been caring for Emmanuel for 6 days and was sorry to see him go. She was also happy he was going to have a family and, especially, a brother. The nurse said the baby ate well, slept well and was not a crier.

Our impression when meeting Emmanuel (now Edward Arthur) was that he was healthy, and had received good care. This impression was confirmed by the nurse's words which, in my opinion, indicated that some bonding between the baby and its caregiver had already taken place. The child's behavior when we brought him home, and for the next year and a half came as a surprise to us.

Let me introduce myself and our family members. We were in the US Foreign Service for 37 years. In that time, we moved 17 times and lived, first as a couple, in ten countries, and then with the children, in eight countries. My husband and I are now retired and our two sons, now 36 and 38 years old have their own lives. They have enthusiastically approved of my idea of writing this book, followed its development and have made several contributions to its content.

We received our first child in the early days of the onset of the Falkland Islands War between Great Britain and Argentina. Because of his job at the US Embassy/Buenos Aires, my husband was part of the US delegation negotiating an end to the confrontation between Argentina and Great Britain. For the first eight days after receiving the baby, we did not see his father.

The description of meeting our children for the first time reveals the fragility of a newborn after the separation from the birth mother, especially if the child has been in a situation of isolation, lacking proper care and affection. These conditions make it necessary for adoptive parents to be sensitive and observant when they receive an adoptive child.

Author's Note

Adoption is a life-changing experience as is the arrival of any child in a family, biological or adopted. Biological parents are in physical and emotional contact with their child during the nine months of pregnancy. They talk to the baby and receive reactions from the baby, especially as the pregnancy advances. By touching the mother's abdomen they can see movements of the fetus. The new life in the womb experiences sounds and other manifestations of the outside world. (Gwen Dewar, Ph.D., 2017-2019.) The biological child and the parents become acquainted with each other before birth. Adoptive parents, however, have struggled with the process of adoption for a long while before realizing their dream of having a child. They are required to go through impersonal, stressful situations and paperwork, all without any contact, physical or emotional, with the child they are to receive.

In this book I propose that nurturing and raising an adopted child requires parental approaches beyond the approaches used by biological parents, and that many children, regardless of the setting where they were before adoption, carry with them emotional wounds caused by the loss of their birth mothers.

These two different situations pre-dispose the parents in each group to differ in the ways they relate to the child. I support this belief based on information obtained by researchers, therapists and our personal experiences.

Adoptive parents, when meeting their son or daughter

for the first time, are consumed by the excitement of the moment. They are unaware that, for the child, there have been physical and psychological events related to the loss of the birth mother. The adopted newborn as well as the adopted older child have lived through the abrupt termination of the on-going, intimate relationship with the birth mother and suddenly find themselves in a vacuum. Placed in an incubator, a hospital crib or in unfamiliar arms, hearing unknown voices and perceiving a different heartbeat, the child is, at a minimum, confused and stressed.

After birth, the biological baby cries or sleeps peacefully, surrounded by familiar voices and smells; I say familiar because the baby has heard the voices and experience the smells in the womb. The adopted child, on the contrary, starts life dealing with distinct circumstances. This child struggles to understand a physiologically and genetically unexpected environment. However, from recent research studies we now know that "there is a biological need that all babies are born with that drives them to bond with their caregivers." (Gwen Dewar, Ph.D., 2017-2019).

I address this subject, in more detail, in the book's section *Knowing and Understanding your Child*, and *Bonding and Attachment*. I also present and analyze the *The Primal Wound* concept (Verrier, Nancy, The Primal Wound, Gateway Press, Inc., Baltimore, MD, 1991), and its effects on a child when separated from the birthmother at birth or soon after.

This first encounter of a child and the adoptive parents marks the beginning of getting to know each other, and learning to trust. As in a biological family, the ways in which the parents react to situations related to their new role as parents will be critical in the process of becoming a family. For both biological and adoptive parents, bonding and attachment ought to be a priority during the first two or three years of life together.

Parenting styles are especially important in the case of Foreign Service and other mobile families. Parents in these families frequently share duties with caregivers in their country of residence and need to be the first line of assistance for their child.

Frequently in today's world, the lives of families are disrupted by events of unrest, war or other circumstances which require separation of the family members. In the case of mobile families such as those in the Foreign Service, missionaries, teachers, students, military personnel, corporate families, researchers and expats, among others, the events surrounding an adoption can be trying. I will address this topic in the last part of the book.

As I discuss all these topics, I will share testimonials, vignettes and anecdotes illustrating the perceptions and feelings of adoptees and their parents, as both adjust to a new life together.

Our contemporary society has defined "typical teen behaviors" referring to developmental behavior patterns found in biological children. Following the same approach, researchers and therapists have identified behavioral manifestations in adopted teenagers and their families. I have taken the liberty to include, in the last part of the book, parental attitudes and methods that have proven useful in facilitating communications and interactions in a family. One of our sons helped me prepare this list of suggestions and titled it "Unsolicited Advice."

I have thought about writing this book for many years. My husband and I had many questions - our children had other questions. We consulted professionals, relied on each other's viewpoints, talked to other parents and read books, trying to grasp the roots of situations we were facing in our family life. Only in the last 10 years have we begun to see more clearly the combination of factors having an impact on our relationships with our sons.

Our first adoption took place after twelve years of marriage. Fortunately, even then, there were the beginnings of services provided by the U.S. Government to support families overseas. The assistance families received when facing crises or difficulties was modest compared to the assistance available today but, nevertheless, it was appreciated.

The book is a non-fiction narrative. This means that no situation, anecdote, information or person in the book was imagined by the author. Identities have been changed when requested, but some names have been kept when approved by the individuals involved.

The main themes of the book are closed adoptions and its consequences, bonding and attachment, the feelings and needs of adoptees, parental approaches towards adopted children and the challenges of adoption in general, and in particular for mobile families. The book does not address adoptions within a foster system, where children are adopted multiple times and/or from one family to another. These adoptions present complications of a different order and require a deeper psychological treatment.

When reflecting about one's life it becomes evident how

impacting certain aspects of the journey have been. It also becomes clear how relevant preparation is when embarking on any project. This clearly applies to adopting a child. In this book I share with readers what our family has learned about creating a nurturing family. Had we known 38 years ago what we now know, our journey would have been equally rich but perhaps less painful, especially for the children. Even after many years, we still struggle at times with the ups and downs of adoption. But we do not love each other less and cherish the many joyful moments we have had as a family.

I would be pleased if this book helps and motivates those who have adopted or are considering adopting, even if all it accomplishes is to expand readers' perception and understanding of an adoption process.

As a final word: The book is not written against adoption. It does talk honestly about the challenges of raising children born into other families. By sharing our experience and the experiences of our many contributors we hope to inspire all those interested in adoption to discover its many facets in order to have a successful journey.

Adoption: A Mosaic of Experiences and Feelings

In the words of a 37-year-old male adoptee speaking to other adoptees:

> "I feel adoption is a special kind of life to be born into. One which requires you to absorb the love from life itself and then cultivate a love of your own within yourself…Yes, we could not count on anyone else for support the moment after birth yet now we reach out and spread love once we find it…Adoption is a life started out with questions and bewilderment …"
>
> — Robert A. Keane, adoptee

Adoption is a life-changing experience for everyone involved, as is the arrival of any child in a family, whether a newborn or an older child.

I am not referring to children who join a family because their parents die in an accident or of a natural cause. Their loss and grief are of a different nature. Children adopted at a later age from homes or orphanages also carry with them emotional wounds but many times react to adoption in a more accepting way. Many times they have seen other children in their institution chosen for adoption, so that, when their turn finally comes, they embrace the opportunity with joy and gratitude.

I am mostly addressing the situation and characteristics of the adoption of a newborn or infant who was separated from the birth mother at the time of birth or soon after.

Introduction

The sum of all experiences in a human being, from the very first signs of life, shapes us as individuals; which we hear, feel, observe, and absorb, our thoughts and desires. Additionally, in the words of an adoptee, the collective memories passed on in each family, form a "generational link" difficult to ignore or break.

If the adopted children are from a different culture, the situation presents additional difficulties. Adoption is not simply "a beautiful gesture." It is a combination of opinions, emotions, feelings, and circumstances intertwined in the lives of the many people who directly or indirectly affect the life of the adoptee.

The role of biological and adoptive parents is to gently accompany a newborn into the future and help the child to thrive physically, adjust socially, and grow psychologically and emotionally.

What circumstances lead a person to become an adoptive parent?

First, there's infertility. There are many reasons why two people are not able to create a new life. This is an extensive topic and I will limit myself to simply include infertility as a common factor leading to adoption. Other circumstances in which adoption occurs are when a same-sex couple desires a family or when a person chooses not to link her or his life to someone else but nevertheless aspires to having children and may see adoption as a solution.

Adoption should not be used as a remedy for a failing marriage.

Secondly, we could speak of Karma, or life turns. As the philosopher Kierkegaard said: "Life can only be understood backwards but it must be lived forwards."

Ideally, before adopting, we need to examine what we are truly looking for in life, to think about our past and our potential future. Once in a while something happens in our lives that leads us in a direction we did not intend to go, creating the foundation for a life we had not envisioned.

Adoption is an event which can transform a life. Its importance cannot be ignored or underestimated. Many roads lead into adoption with as many diverse outcomes. There is no "one size fits all." The ending of each adoption story depends on a multitude of factors.

Adoption should be taken as an act of love; yes, love is a major component. Yet, adoption is so much more; in addition to feelings and emotions, there are legal procedures, questions which cannot be answered, social interactions, and acceptances or rejections which will be present throughout the family's journey.

PART ONE

In Retrospect

I WOULD LIKE to review the circumstances leading to our choice for adoption. If you are considering adopting, reflect on your own life as you read along, think of possible transitional moments in your own journey. Use this time to reflect on your personal circumstances, visions of the future, dreams, wishes and desires.

My life experience did not take me from high school into marriage, as was common at the time. Instead, I chose to attend a two year, college-level program to become an executive bilingual secretary. As it happened, the reward given by the secretarial school to the graduating student with the best academic record was a scholarship to study in Madrid, Spain. I was the one chosen the year of my graduation and I jumped at the opportunity. I applied to study Sociology. It turned out that the place of study was an institute of Religious Social Studies where I was the only student not belonging to a religious order (i.e., priest, nun, monk or pastor).

After a year trying to function in this unexpected environment I decided to decline the scholarship. Instead, with some friends, I moved to London with the intention of spending the summer learning English as a Second Language, (ESL). I reasoned this would be a good way to complement my language skills for an eventual secretarial job. That was my plan…

I traveled to England through an organization which assisted international students in securing a job as an Au Pair while at the same time enrolling them to study a new language.

One day, while strolling in London with another Au Pair, my friend Ana, I simply suddenly collapsed on the sidewalk with intense abdominal cramps. Alarmed, Ana hailed a taxi which drove us to the nearest hospital. I had suffered terrible pains since I matured, but none of the adults in my family, several of them medical doctors, recognized the symptoms as requiring attention or treatment. After a careful examination, the emergency room doctor explained the possible cause of my pains and collapse was the bursting of cysts in my abdominal area, produced by many years of the undiscovered endometriosis condition. At the time, the only treatment for the condition was surgery. In order to prevent a generalized abdominal infection, I was immediately transferred to surgery.

I survived the ordeal thanks to the help of several dear friends, with whom I remain in touch until today, and to the generosity of the British National Health System. In those days the United Kingdom considered foreign students to be guests of the country and they covered all the expenses of my hospitalization and recovery. I am forever grateful to them.

My post-surgery situation made it impossible for me to continue working as an Au Pair. I needed to find a place to live and recover and I needed to engage in a different type of activity.

Soon after my arrival in London I connected with a couple, Mr. and Mrs. Duron, the aunt and uncle of a student I had met in Madrid. Mr. and Mrs. Duron were from Honduras. They had lived in London for many years because of Mr. Duron's position as the Permanent Representative of the Government of Honduras to the United Kingdom. Mrs.

Duron was a warm, perceptive and generous woman who promptly understood my situation and helped me find a room to rent in a basement flat, just a few houses from her home. We frequently saw each other. She soon recognized I was struggling to communicate in English; I could understand the language but my speaking ability was not good. Mrs. Duron suggested if I wanted to learn English well, I should focus my studies on anything but English. As she explained, if I took classes on a subject matter native speakers were likely to study, I would be surrounded by English speakers instead of being surrounded by foreigners like me, all making the same grammatical mistakes.

I thought her advice made a lot of sense and enrolled in a one-year program at St. Nicholas Training Center, an institution founded by an Italian educator and physician, Maria Montessori, for training adults in the philosophy and methodology of her approach to educating children.

I have since learned that the Montessori methodology is not appropriate for all children. It is particularly controversial regarding children with sensorial disabilities. In my case, it offered a good foundation for understanding children as a teacher and as a parent.

While I studied, I was fortunate to have a position as a caregiver for a two-year- old child, the son of a Bolivian family, friends of mine. The family generously accommodated my circumstances. We remain friends today. Their son is now an adult and a successful sculptor, and I keep the memory of them close to my heart, enriched by occasional telephone calls or a trip to London.

After I felt strong and healthy enough to travel, I took an

Italian ship, The Rossini, for a ten day trip back to Colombia. I had been away from home for three and a half years and became quite emotional when I saw my mother and sister waiting for me at the harbor. Back then, there were no cell phones, no What's App, no FedEx and it took three months for a letter to go from South America to Europe. I was eager to see my folks again and to hear some news from home.

Once back in Colombia, my country of origin, I did what I usually do when facing difficulties: I decided to "grab the bull by the horns" and move on with my life.

I decided not to let the little dirty word, "infertility" ruin my life. I worked as a kindergarten teacher in a bilingual school in Bogota, enrolled at the university and eventually, completed a B.A in Psychology from a Colombian university and Indiana University in the USA. Later on, I obtained a Master of Arts in Education from George Washington University in Washington, D.C.

Between studies, trips and other distractions, I met my husband who was a Peace Corps Volunteer in my hometown. He was only 23 years old but so much more mature than other men I knew. I was impressed by his self-confidence and his desire to help others. When he started to invite me out for dates I told him point blank that I was unable to have children. He simply said: "I am not looking for a baby factory but for a companion for my life." Well, that sealed the deal. We became good friends at first and four years later, we married.

We started a life in the United States Foreign Service which took us to several countries. Our third assignment was to Argentina, the country of origin of our two sons.

Our Adoption Experience

AFTER 12 YEARS of marriage, my husband and I decided that we wanted to start a family. We inquired about possibilities for adoption in Buenos Aires, Argentina, where we were living. Argentina only offers closed adoptions and, at that time, knowing as little as we did about adoptions, we did not think it would be an obstacle and proceeded to apply for a child. Closed adoptions means that parents receiving a child are not given any information about the birth mother, her pregnancy, birth experience, place of birth, or extended family. As I will explain later in the book this situation has several repercussions for the adoptees later in life.

After a little more than a year of submitting applications and surviving numerous home visits, interviews with psychiatrists, social workers and psychologists, all trying to decide if we would be responsible, caring parents, we were told to wait for a call from a social worker. Mrs. Cosme's call came on a Friday afternoon and the rest is history, as the saying goes. We went on to successfully complete two adoptions in two-and-a-half years.

My husband and I started our adoption journey assured that there was no difference between raising a biological child and an adopted child. All we would need to do was to take the child home and offer lots of love, good nutrition and a good education. We heard this message from counselors, psychologists, and books, and were convinced, yes, this was all we had to do. This notion is so far from the reality of our experience! We now know there is much more to consider and do to become a healthy adoptive family and to successfully launch the children into their adult lives.

One lesson my husband and I have learned from our experience with adoption is that in order to effectively support our children's growth toward a positive self-identity, adoptive parents need to *know, understand and* accept how what transpired in our children's earlier life affects them as they mature.

As mentioned at the beginning of the book, the circumstances of meeting our adopted sons could not have been more different. If one is to believe the theories of trauma from the separation from a biological mother, and I do believe them, our second son appeared to already have formed an attachment to the nurse caring for him. He ate well, slept well, was gaining weight and seemed calm and relaxed. However, when we brought him home he began to have an irregular schedule, had difficulties sleeping, and was eating in excess. He developed a persistent diarrhea which lasted for almost a year and a half. Physical symptoms are common manifestations of trauma, stress and anxiety.

Through vignettes and anecdotes from our lives and the lives of other adopting families and adoptees, I will illustrate possible behavioral manifestations in some adoptees due to the turmoil operating in a child's inner life as a result of the separation from the birth mother or other complicating circumstances which may come up throughout the child's life.

I will also address how the family may face many situations in their lifetime which will require adaptation and, most important, acceptance. Sometimes expectations have to be revised and toned down. Parents will be wise not to forget that their adopted child has a hereditary past that pulls him into a different direction, interests or inclinations.

The Keane family

Knowing Yourself, Knowing Your Child

Sometimes, in adoption, we need to welcome what the children embrace and choose for their lives, due to their personality and inherited traits, and not what we envision for them.

Every child is born with what used to be called "*elan vital*," or life force, what researchers today call a "drive," which pushes a child to bond with a caregiver. Today's researchers describe this drive as an intense concentration on the part of a baby to capture every movement, action, visual effect, sound and touch coming from his or her surrounding environment. (Gwen Dewar, Ph.D., 2017-2019).

The Montessori methodology, but specially its philosophy, prepares teachers and caregivers to develop and exercise four important skills, very necessary when attending to young children.

- Observation
- Sensitivity
- Accommodation and flexibility
- Patience

Observation of people's behaviors; sensitivity to people's needs and feelings; accommodation beyond one's preferences to what a person needs or seems to need, allowing choices; and patience and tolerance. Translated into today's jargon, we can say that the Montessori philosophy prepares one to be mindful, to adapt to a changing world and daily demands, and to allow events and situations to develop before reacting or overreacting.

Montessori's educational philosophy proposes during the first years of life, from birth to about six years of age, the child responds to "an *inner teacher*," her words, who acts automatically to satisfy all the child's developmental needs. We have all observed how a little child goes about the day minding his own business: sits here or there; talks to himself; walks around touching things for no apparent reason; or stands still for long periods, apparently doing nothing.

Dr. Montessori's philosophical position was based on her medical training and long hours of observations of small children in pre-schools in impoverished sections of Rome. She states that a child is, during the first years, very busy "absorbing the environment," (her term) and learning from it. All systems and senses are engaged. The adult's role is to provide a safe and stimulating environment and to act as a facilitator around the child. During these years, the child follows her "inner teacher" to develop skills in several specific areas of development. As soon as the child realizes she has perfected the necessary skills in one area, she moves on to the next, in a strict order of developmental laws.

A question which arises for adoptive parents is what happens when a child is adopted and begins to live in an environment very different to the environment where the child was conceived, born and genetically pre-programmed to experience?

This is where the *biological drive* comes into play. This innate drive opens a path and an opportunity for the adoptive parents to connect and bond with their children, when they assume the role of caregivers in the absence of the birthmother. This is very good news for adoptive parents.

PART TWO

From the Uterus to the Arms of Strangers: The Primal Wound

THE PRIMAL WOUND: Understanding the Adopted Child, by Nancy Newton Verrier, describes how a child can possibly feel when separated from the biological mother at birth. Ms. Verrier, a psychologist, therapist and mother of a biological child and an adopted child, says:

> What I discovered is what I call the *primal wound,*
> a wound which is physical, emotional, psychological,
> and spiritual; a wound which causes pain so profound as
> to have been described as cellular by those adoptees who
> allowed themselves to go that deeply into their pain.

Ms. Verrier continues to say, "I began to understand this wound as having been caused by the separation of the child from his biological mother, the connection to whom seems mystical, mysterious, spiritual and everlasting."

This reaction is, by no means, universal. Some adoptees grow without having experienced such pain or without feeling the need to go deeper into their feelings; they even describe themselves as having been "happy babies." This might be the case with many adoptees, at least until the age when they fully understand the meaning of motherhood and the loss adoption brought with it.

The Primal Wound was the initial basis for my belief, given the early experiences of a child, parenting adopted children requires additional approaches, not instead of, but in addition to, the customary parenting methods in a society.

In our adoption, given the evident changes our children

were exhibiting, especially as they approached puberty, the importance of the mother/child relationship and Ms. Verrier's insights impacted me in such a way that I started to review my relationship with them, my role as their mother and our family's style of communication. I began to realize the many vacuums and missteps throughout our parental roles were due, in part, to our lack of experience in the area of parenting but also due to the many times we needed to relocate from country to country. In reconsidering our parental roles and approaches, the effect multiple separations could have on the children needed to be taken into account in order to understand and support them. We were all forced by the circumstances to adjust and re-adjust to multiple differing situations, to develop new habits, friendships, activities and interests, to learn under different school systems and educational programs and sometimes in a foreign language; and to be able to function without the links we had established in previous places of residence. At every new country or city, the children were forced to start creating new connections which, based on my experience as an adult living through, not equal but similar circumstances, is an exhausting exercise.

Today we call the ability to adjust to these multiple changes, *resilience*.

The narrative included at the beginning of the book regarding meeting our children for the first time represents some of the conditions adopting parents experience when meeting their children. Parents, in general, are excited about receiving a child. For biological parents, the long nine month wait is over. For adoptive parents, this moment is of particular relevance. Not having experienced the months of pregnancy to become one with the child, the adoptive parents also react with excitement, holding their much desired child; but they are not aware of the circumstances that brought the child to adoption, the experiences the child has gone through after the separation from the birth mother or the possible multiple memories and imprints left in the child's brain and psyche. (Gwen Dewar, Ph.D., 2017-2019)

We can call this part of the adoption process the beginning of the adventure for parents and children. It marks the start of a long journey on the road to becoming a family, getting to know and trust each other. For the child, this moment is the first step towards finding a new place in the world. Keep in mind that an adoptee has not only lost a birth mother; adoptees also lose an extended family, a culture and with it, that culture's music, arts, language and history. All roots and connections have been broken.

We were not aware of the reason for these diverse reactions of the children once they came to our family. We had received some advice about how to manage newborns, feedings, diaper changes, sleep schedules, the common knowledge stuff. We were far from understanding the children's behaviors could be manifestations of an internal struggle they could be going through, when encountering a reality that was quite different from the one they were genetically programmed to experience.

This is where bonding and attachment come in. The child's situation is not pre-determined to be permanent and absolute. The newborn or young child does not have to remain in a state of confusion about her new life. This is where the well -prepared adoptive parents also come in, ready to start their task of establishing a positive relationship with their children, helping them feel comfortable at their new home, and thriving in their new, unexpected environment.

When a child is separated from its mother at birth, or a few hours or days later, the child finds herself in a physical, sensorial and psychological empty space.

A newborn child is programmed to search for the mother he has been connected with during nine months of pregnancy. Most of its senses are operational.

This means a baby exhibits automatic, species genetically programmed responses to sensorial stimulation, responses which have existed for millennia to help humankind survive. These responses come from the ability to see, smell, feel, taste, and hear, and from the baby's programmed need to survive by attracting the attention of the caregiver. Research shows that during the first weeks of life, a newborn reacts to the smell of its mother's milk while any other substance put in his mouth will produce a grimace. A baby also exhibits strong reflex movements to all kinds of touch and, contrary to a common belief, babies feel pain. A newborn's eyes are fully formed but the eye muscles are still learning to work together; a baby's preferred subjects are faces, especially the mother's face, and the contrast of light and dark and objects in motion. Babies hear many diverse sounds and react to them accordingly, but the one sound they recognize and react to fastest is the mother's voice and human voices in general. [Source, among others, Penelope Leach, "The Essential First Year", 2010]; Maria Montessori, "The Absorbent Mind" early 20th century, Several books on Bonding and Attachment, Gwen Dewar, Ph.D., 1017-1019)

Biologically speaking, this situation is not very different from that of a baby kangaroo searching for its mother's pouch immediately after birth.

Like the baby kangaroo, the newborn child is programmed to search for sounds, a heartbeat, and most importantly, the smell of the mother's milk. Most of us have seen a pregnant mother showing someone how her baby reacts, in the uterus, when she talks to the unborn baby or taps er abdomen.

When born, a child feels the need to immediately establish physical contact with the mother; not a nurse or an incubator or a crib and a bottle. The newborn is yet unable to verbalize reactions and feelings to the vacuum it is experiencing. He/she is struggling to find something that is not there. Not only does the child find herself in an unexpected situation but s/he feels the impact of being in the arms of unfamiliar people. The child is feeling the shock of the interruption of the physical and psychological process of bonding s/he is programmed to experience. The child cannot control or correct the situation. He/she can only react organically, absorbing the feelings of stress which produce confusion. Contrast the feelings of the happy adoptive parents welcoming the much-desired child and the state of internal turmoil of the child separated from the birth mother. In addition to the natural impact of the birth experience, the child is required to negotiate another difficult situation: the abrupt or gradual separation from the birthmother.

The manifestations of all this stress vary. Some babies cry and fuss; others show anger; some refuse to eat, or are unable to sleep; others develop skin rashes, diarrhea or other physical manifestations. Some others might not show signs of distress until later on, sometimes not until adolescence.

When I shared the *Primal Wound* concept with our two sons they said, as have been said by many adoptees, "No wonder I always felt like I did not belong in this family." One son gave a more concise response: "It resonates."

Complexities of Adoption

Our sons were told very early in life about being adopted. There was evidence and affirmation of our love all along in their lives, photo albums, stories, celebrations. However, according to our sons and other adoptees there is always a dissonant feeling of "Why am I here?"; "Why do I feel this way?"; "I love my parents but…"

When adoptees were asked the question: "What influence has adoption had in your life?

Adoptee "A", 80 yrs. old, said, "I have always been very insecure. I still am…"

Adoptee "R", 34 years old, said, "For a long time I never thought adoption was an issue in my identity…Looking back, I see that it actually did have some lasting effects on me, subconsciously…It was more of a deep feeling, of not fitting in…"

Adoptee "D" said, "It's a different type of loneliness."

Adoptee "S" said, "For me it was always the question: Who am I? Because I was very different from my adopted parents and sister."

As quoted in Sherrie Eldridge's book, *Twenty Things Adopted Kids Wish Their Adoptive Parents Knew*, psychologists Joseph Luft and Harry Ingram conclude there are four dimensions of an individual's identity:

One dimension is what that individual knows about the self; another, just as real, *what the person does not know about him or herself*; the third dimension is what other people know about the person; a fourth *is what the person hides from others.*

Of these four dimensions the ones of most interest to adoptive parents are the second and fourth. These components of an identity are the ones the adoptee chooses not to share with others and the part that makes necessary for adoptive parents to be not just loving protectors and advocates but also a little bit of a detective. How do we penetrate that fourth dimension? How do we get our children to share with us that carefully guarded inner core of their identity, of their true feelings?

A mother tells about the day her adopted daughter graduated from high school. While embracing her daughter after receiving the diploma she had asked:

"Did you think of your biological mother today?" The girl replied: "I think of her every day, Mom."

For some adoptees, the image of their biological mother is always in their minds. For other adoptees, her image comes and goes, at different stages of life. The birth mother's image becomes more prevalent during the puberty years, when the adoptee understands motherhood and procreation; or when the adoptive parents express concerns to the adoptee that the birth mother might come at any time and take the child away from them.

Adopted children have a perspective which differs from that of children raised by biological parents. They have needs and a logic that agrees with their unconscious perception of their beginnings. Biological children do not have to worry themselves about aspects of their life such as: Who was my mother? Or, was my mother a drug addict? Was she raped? What did my mother look like?

When one of our sons was ten and a half years old, he

expressed a desire to find his biological family. I explained to him about closed adoptions, that we had not been given any information about his biological family, but, I said, we could send a letter to the agency in Buenos Aires which had processed the adoption. He liked this idea and agreed to do it. I suggested he give me some ideas of what he wanted to say in the letter and this is what he told me to write:

"I am ten and a half years old and I wonder where my mother is, what was her name, what she looked like, why she gave me up for adoption, if I had brothers and sisters, what are their names, if I had a dad, if they gave up my brothers and sisters too, if she is still alive, if you can say hi to her. If I can arrange to see her I will go back there…"

My reaction: WOW!

This came to nothing because the agency responded, as they usually do in closed adoptions, that the records for the year the child had been adopted had been burnt. I personally I consider this response the epitome of cruelty and dishonesty. I wonder how our son and other adoptees felt when given this answer.

In the United States a common situation adoptees face is being told that to release the records of their adoption a judge's decision is necessary. Sometimes the search leads the adoptee down the wrong path when the information about place or date of birth have been intentionally changed.

As a side note, I want to mention, at least in the United States, some adoption agencies offer the birth mother the option to sign a document, to be placed in the adoptee's records, which authorizes the child to search for the birth mother. This document contains addresses or phone numbers where the birthmother can be located. Some birthmothers update this document as the years pass, others do not, based on their personal circumstances. It is good to keep this option in mind when adopting.

As adoptive parents, we face situations like this but there is not much we can do to help. However, it is necessary for us to know that there is an inner self in our children we need to reach in whatever way we can. These and other conditions program adoptees to be secretive, restrained, to protect their feelings and emotions and, sometimes, to distrust anyone and everything around them. Think about it: if you cannot trust your birth mother because, after all, she abandoned you, who can you trust?

Maria Montessori wrote in her book *The Absorbent Mind:*

"From the moment of birth the child is incorporating his environment into his psyche and his physical being. The child needs to make constant accommodations to unify what his genetic inheritance is telling him to find and the experiences he is living."

This dichotomy makes it necessary for the child to deal with undertones and aspects of a different situation and sometimes a different culture. Simultaneously, the adults are trying to familiarize themselves with the child.

This leads me to believe adopted children see the adopted family through a particular lens. And of course they are right, from their point of view. Later on, these circumstances create a conflict when adoptees begin to look at adoption in a deeper sense, with more conscious and critical eyes. They begin to reject a great deal of their lives to that point and feel at odds with their families, but at the same time they feel they love their adoptive parents and feel distressed when they exhibit certain behaviors they themselves do not understand. According to Rachel Staff, author of "Parenting Adopted Teenagers," (Jessica Kinsley Publishers, London and Philadelphia, 2016), this confronting of adoption from a different point of view usually begins around eleven or twelve years of age. This is the age when most children begin to understand procreation, motherhood, genetic influences, and other aspects they had not considered until then.

As expressed by an adoptee, age 36, reflecting on being adopted:

"I had on my own come to conclude that I had abandonment and rejection issues on a deeper level, unresolved and transformed into anger..."

Hours, days, weeks, or months after the child is born, the adopting parents come into his life. They are full of expectations and love for a child they have been trying in earnest to receive. The parents have been told by books and well-meaning people all that is needed is a home, a cheerful room, lots of love and attention and good care. And sometimes, this is enough to help a child adapt to a new home. In my research and interviews I have heard many heartening narratives about successful adoptions as expressed by the parents or the adoptees themselves. But many other times parents are baffled when their son or daughter refuses to respond to attempts to love them. No matter what the new parents do, the child does not sleep well, eat, or simply does not thrive, rejects physical contact or seems removed, or absent, indifferent. As one author of a book on adoption, said, "I was more than ready to love my daughter but she was not ready to be loved."

Other young adoptees do not exhibit symptoms until later. Adopting parents talk about unusual behaviors of their little ones, at one, two or three years of age,

"He would get up after I put him to sleep and after I had gone to bed myself. He would come and place himself in the doorway of our bedroom and go to sleep there. If I put him back in his bed, he would come back to our door over and over again until we finally opted for letting him sleep with us."

"At age three, our child would have terrible nightmares; we would wake up to his screams, rush to his room and found him sitting in bed, with eyes open, but screaming and sound asleep; it would take a great deal of effort to wake him up, carry him to the bathroom, wash his face, talk to him, but nothing seemed to help. As he continued to grow he was constantly worried about being lost, about being left behind." Our oldest, when he was around 3 years old, and had to go to the bathroom in a public place with toilet stalls would ask me to stand just outside, very close to the door so he could see my shoes and would ask me constantly, "Are you still there, Mom?"

You could be shaking your head, thinking, "But many biological children do these things also…" This is true, but the difference is *in the intensity and the length of the episodes, the anguish and desperation shown by the child.*

Even so, not all adopted children react the same way under equal circumstances. Our first son, as he himself expresses, panicked whenever he feared being lost or abandoned. Our second son, in contrast, never showed any concern about being lost. Once, during a trip to London when Edward was about six years old, he disappeared from our side at the British Museum. If you are not familiar with this museum, it is huge. We panicked, called the guards, looked here, looked there for him, the alarms went on. All of a sudden I heard his voice, "Mom, come here," and I saw him peeking out from behind one of the display cabinets. In great exasperation, but very relieved, I said, "Edward, where were you? You were lost…we were worried!" And he said, "I was not lost, you were lost; I knew where I was." Yes, a smile is in order…The point is, parents need to learn to see behaviors from different angles and respond accordingly; much more so when dealing with the unknowns in the life of an adoptee.

An adoptee, a friend of ours, said the following when talking about adoptee's behaviors:

"I believe there is a wide range of situations, going from adoptees who are obsessed and frustrated because of the separation from the birth mother and their inability to find their biological parents, to those like me, curious and frustrated but not agonizing, to others who could care less…" Steve C.

I consider this to be a valid observation, and I would like to add to the last sentence, *who appear to care* less. Do not forget there is an aspect in the personality of adoptees, validated by many adoptees and by researchers and therapists, regarding the complex psychology of some adoptees.

Many adult adoptees who are able to talk about their experience mention feeling restless, a constant need to search, to question, to test their parents' love.

They do not understand these could be, in a worst case scenario, the manifestations of the impact of the loss of the birth mother. They might have no memory of it, cannot understand their feelings, but this separation left an imprint within them which has manifested and will manifest in different ways as they grow. Even if they do not have a memory of the moment itself, society is constantly reminding us of the importance and value of motherhood. Adoptees would need to live in a space capsule to miss this emphasis on motherhood and therefore not ever think and question why they were given up for adoption by their own mothers.

Common reactions reported by adoptees troubled by the facts of adoption and by many researchers and therapists are: constant, unexplained anger, unjustified fears, fear of rejection, testing behaviors, aggression towards the adoptive parents or siblings whom they love, acting out in the neighborhood, at school, in any social group and other reported behaviors such as depressions, addictions and suicide attempts. Our son Robert, now an adult, expresses it this way:

> "A rebellious nature blossomed inside me from a frustrated space in which I felt no one understood me. Sounds like a redundant " teen cliché" but I now see it as an alienation from my entire family…I didn't share their outlook in life, religion, politics, humor, music preferences and so on."

Many people prefer to adopt newborns or very young children to diminish the impact of adoption on the child. This is logical; the younger the child is, the more time the adoptive parents have to form a healthy attachment.

Part Two

Opening up the subject of adoption as early as possible or when the first opportunity arises will help establish an atmosphere of trust between parents and child, a link for future relationships and conversations. I have been told by adoptees how devastating it is for them to learn, accidentally, about being adopted. The most common feeling is, "I now realize that my parents have been lying to me all these years."

I will now address bonding and attachment and other aspects of parenting, in general, and especially parenting adopted children.

PART THREE

Bonding and Attachment

CHILD DEVELOPMENT SPECIALISTS say the years between the pre-natal stage and birth to three years of age are the most critical years for a child, especially in an adoption situation. A biological child has been exposed in her pre-natal life to sensations and feelings which remain some place in the memory. For example, the home situation of the mother or parents, their relationship, an excess of stress or negative feelings, all impact the unborn child to the extent that her heart rate changes as well as the level of cortisone in its system when placed under the situations mentioned above. These factors even affect the development of the right hemisphere of the brain, according to researchers in the field. Authors Karin B. Purvis PH.D and David R. Cross, Ph.D., in their book *The Connected Child* explain how important body and brain functions are controlled by substances called neurotransmitters. They state:

> "Vulnerable, at-risk children can have neurotransmitter systems that remain hyper-aroused, making them less resilient to stress over time. The more anxious the child feels, the more s/he reactivates old traumas, which in turn releases neurotransmitters that make them increasingly aggressive and belligerent or unreasonable."

One adoptee, responding to this segment of the book said:

> "This section resonates with me in recalling that I was an anxious kid, too easily upset and offended,

and frustrated by my limited ability to make and keep friends, i.e., always feeling like an outsider. It took years to grow out of that. How much this can be related to my pre-birth conditions I cannot guess, but certainly my adoptive home did not help. Ours was not a happy household."

Bonding is something which occurs naturally between a baby and the birth mother through the process of intimate communication during the pregnancy and birth but is absent between the adoptee and its new parents when they first become acquainted.

Attachment means togetherness, mutual understanding and flowing communication with positive experiences, a sense of belonging and security. In the case of a mother or caregiver and a young child (0 to 3 years of age) a positive bonding and attachment also refers to the feelings elicited by interaction between caregiver and child; it could be gestures, actions, sounds or words to which the caregiver/mother reacts in a positive way. Of interest to those who would like to go further into this topic I suggest reviewing Bethany Saltman's book, *Strange Situation,* Ballantine, 2020.

Attachment exists among the members of a family in varying degrees. It exists between the members of couples, between teenagers in friendship or love and between parents and children. Attachment is a slow process and it begins in the womb.

Some authors talk about the difference between a simple bonding, that is, "getting along just fine, thank you" - and a secure, positive attachment. The words "positive attachment" imply an emotional connection between caregiver and child, which continues beyond the first years. In simple terms, a positive connection with your child means being and feeling "plugged in" to a child's needs, beyond attending to the daily physical needs such as feeding, bathing the baby, providing a place to sleep, etc. The caregiver "reads and interprets" the child's body signals. For example: our first child, when he was about one year old, started doing something we found curious: he would put the weight of his body on his head and the ball of his feet, lift the middle of his body and arch. We could not understand what he was doing. After a while we concluded that he did that mostly at the end of the day and when he was tired. So we started taking his arching as a sign that he was ready for bed. Another interesting clue the children gave us when they were tired was to lead us to the sound system and say "music?" He and his brother had learned we listened to music and read books to them just before bedtime.

Attachment and bonding are a highly sensorial interplay of exchanges between a child and parents, adoptive parents or caregiving adults. Attachment grows, in a positive way, as the interactions increase. It involves all senses and psychological emotions or moods. During the first months of a baby's life, newly out of the womb, these exchanges are more frequent, more focused. Eye contact, skin contact, cooing, music and sounds, and a pleasant, warm environment free of stress, maximizes the child's perception of belonging and safety. This environment nurtures physical, psychological and essential brain development. Each time a child is held, rocked, fed, spoken to or smiled at, adds one more link of positive attachment. Psychologists believe this bonding at an early age sets the stage for a child to feel comfortable in close relationships later in life and facilitates the formation of trust.

For a mobile family adopting a child overseas bonding and attachment are of special relevance. If both parents work outside the house, the child may also form some attachment with another adult caregiver while the parents are away from home. The parents would be wise to avoid multiple or frequent changes in caregivers in order to diminish the effect of separations and reconnecting on the part of the child.

In the Foreign Service, in particular, parents need to keep in mind these periods of adjustment in their life with an adopted child when they plan their assignments.

From the early years of interest in theories of attachment (M. Ainsworth, 1913-1999), passing through John Bowlby's (1907-1999) three-volume masterpiece, *Attachment and Loss*, through the many publications, YouTube videos, online presentations and the counseling of today, developmental psychologists have been exploring the subject of Attachment from many different angles for years.

The good news out of this jungle of information is there are ways to help an adopted child adjust to the new unfamiliar environment. But it is necessary to detect the clues and signs the baby is giving of discomfort, anxiety, or emotional upset. A calm, relaxed baby requires a calm and relaxed caregiver.

It is important to keep in mind an adoptive parent bringing home a child born in a foreign country has to juggle two parallel processes: playing the supportive role of helping the child interact with and learn from the new environment, while at the same time gently establishing a good bond and attachment with the child.

During these critical times of parents and adoptees getting acquainted, it is of particular importance for families to manage stress.

The influence of stress on a person or family life is very much discussed today. We all read about stressors in our lives, how to avoid them, and how to reduce them. "Mindfulness" is the "in" word of our times; exercise, meditation, yoga, Zen, are words we hear and read about on daily basis. So there is no need to cover stress extensively, its causes and symptoms; I will limit myself to a few remarks on aspects I consider of the upmost importance.

Stress is the body and mind's reaction to anything a person perceives to be a threat. ("The Science of Stress", Time Magazine, 2020). Perception is very personal; what creates stress for one person can go unnoticed by another. Stress is normal in our lives. It can help prevent accidents, motivate or keep a person going. If not properly managed, if it becomes chronic and persistent, it produces constant anxiety which will eventually affect the person's health and mind.

A recent study at Harvard University (https://www.pbs. org/newshour/show/why-reducing-a-pregnant-womans-toxic-stress-can-improve-the-health-of-her-unborn-child) researched single, pregnant young women who, during the months of pregnancy, had to struggle to survive without help from the baby's father or other family members. The researchers designed experimental situations to observe stress in the child. Reactions of the child seen through a double sided mirror revealed hyperactivity, expressions of discomfort, inappropriate social behaviors, excessive crying, tantrums, slow speech and excessive clinging towards adults. The study showed the results of the pre-natal stress of the mother had been transmitted to the unborn child. Unknowingly, the stressed mother can easily create an inconsistent, hit or miss process of negative interactions, failure to communicate, unpredictable behaviors and responses resulting in a much stressed baby.

The negative interactions produce uneasy feelings in the parent/child relationship and eventually begin to breed mistrust. If interactions between two people are mostly unsatisfactory, emotionally painful, and sad or negative, the process of attachment suffers and the people interacting begin to pull apart. Where the interactions produce anxiety and uneasiness the bond breaks rather than enriches the connection.

Some symptoms of stress are observable, such as hyperactivity, irritability, excessive talking, excessive eating, and insomnia. Others may go unnoticed even by the person suffering them: feeling overwhelmed, racing thoughts, irregular sleep patterns, difficulties concentrating, memory loss, constantly worrying, among others.

Young children, when faced with unpredictable, unmanageable situations, express their discomfort (stress) in different ways. They fuss, cry for no apparent reason, become angry or irritable, refuse to eat and develop digestion problems, skin conditions, even a low grade fever. Nightmares and excessive fears are also common signs of stress in children.

In the case of adoptive children and their adoptive

parents, some factors can interfere with a healthy development of attachment. If the birth mother had been a substance user or under extreme stress during the pregnancy or involved in a violent domestic situation, the baby might look perfectly healthy but could eventually show signs of anxiety, developmental delays, or a general inability to thrive. The child may be indifferent and emotionally removed from a situation or reject touch or other social interactions, tend to be over-reactive, and sleep and eat poorly. In general, the child would be an unresponsive child.

For a more comprehensive coverage of this subject please visit: Helpguide.org/articles/parenting-family/what-is-secure-attachment-and-bonding-htm.

You may want to sign up to receive their newsletter.

Attachment does not happen suddenly or fast. It's a continuous, evolving process; the baby constantly elicits behaviors from the environment and the caregivers based on an innate, sensorial urge for protection which is believed to exist to guarantee the survival of the species and is seen in both human babies as well as animals. It is a circular process during which the child's behavior provokes a reaction from the caregiver and, at the same time, the caregiver's actions and behaviors elicit actions and emotion in the child. If the bonding process is healthy and positive, internal models formed within the child will influence all future interactions with the world. Continuing positive interactions lead to an attitude of trust, confidence and a healthy self-esteem. Life is okay, the baby concludes; these people like me, I trust them.

If the interactions are frustrating and anxiety producing for all parties, it can lead to a model of behavior which programs the child to generally expect ill feelings, harsh conditions, harsh treatment, or, many times, indifference. Along with this comes insecurity, an overall attitude of distrust of the surrounding environment. The child reacts either with self-defense behaviors (crying, tantrums), or with behaviors of rejection of the caregiver such as physical or emotional avoidance, excessive compliance or disengaging with the immediate world.

Parents who adopt older children and who therefore did not have the opportunity to promote a close relationship with the child in the early years have a more complex task of nurturing a bond to encourage relating. This does not mean they should think bonding and attachment are impossible. The process of attachment is ongoing and fluid. The more the parents can learn about the life of the child prior to meeting them, the easier the task of initiating attachment and bonding. The parents need to observe, interpret, guess, and react appropriately to each behavior the child exhibits. They need to ask themselves multiple questions: what do I know about this child? What was the immediate environment in her life prior to coming to us? What language did the child hear? What other people were around the child: siblings, cousins, neighbors? Did the child have any toys? Were there any illnesses in the family for which the child was left to his own devices? Did the child lack good nutrition? And on and on, as much as the parent's imagination can provide.

Regardless of the age of the child, the parents need to initiate the task of incrementing physical proximity, as the child gives signs of accepting physical touch or proximity of the parents. When children have lived in abusive environments, or in deprived situations like living in an orphanage or even on the streets, or under intense isolation and removed from human contact, they will manifest internal uneasiness, pain, fears and frustrations by means of rebellious reactions, rejection of physical proximity, verbal abuse, tantrums, running away from home and many more actions intended to express their discomfort.

Physical contact like skin to skin (holding hands, for example) eye to eye contact, talking to the child while feeding, changing diapers, bathing, playing times, using simple, short words the child will begin to recognize, repeating the sounds the child makes, even if meaningless, will lead to situations that will feel rewarding for both parent and child. These simple interactions will lead the child to experience happy moments with adults. An indication that you are doing the right things to bond with your child will be that you will find yourself so much in love with this child that it hurts, and you will look for opportunities to spend time in closeness with the child instead of agonizing about every small interaction.

I have mentioned a number of the most observable and distinguishing behaviors which describe the process and results of attachment and bonding but for a more comprehensive treatment of the subject and for addressing a more therapeutic approach to corrective behaviors I recommend reading *The Connected Child* by Karyn B. Purvis, Ph.D., and David R. Cross, Ph.D. This book and many other current books offered through internet sources (as mentioned in the bibliography), magazines, adoption services and sites, therapists, provide a wealth of tested situations which, for an adoptive parent, are a helpful guide into the unknown.

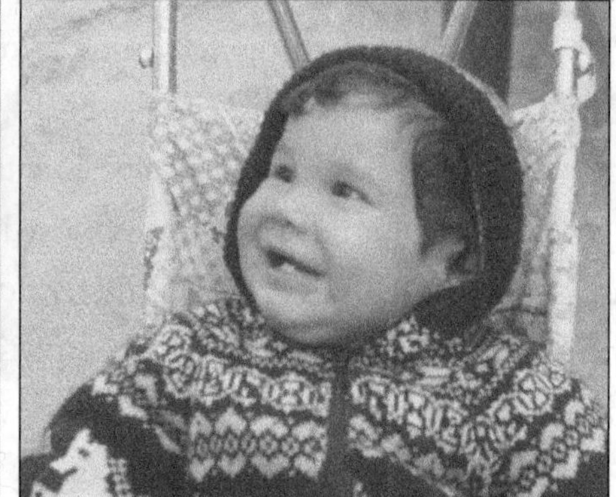

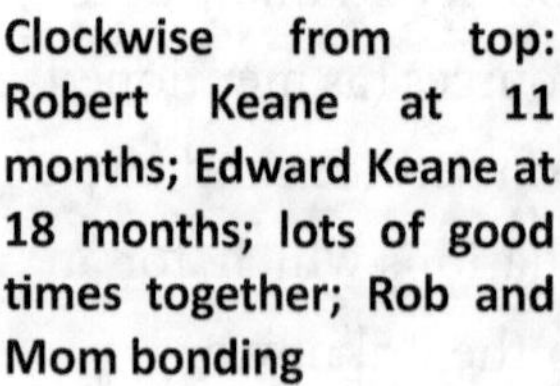

Clockwise from top: Robert Keane at 11 months; Edward Keane at 18 months; lots of good times together; Rob and Mom bonding

Clockwise from top left: Ed and Dad bonding; the Keane's male gang; Robert and Ed with Grandpa and Grandma; with Abuelita Matilde

The Golden Years of Adoption, Ages Three to Eleven

WHILE LIVING IN Brasilia, we were lucky to have a large house, with several rooms and bathrooms. Our children immediately concluded that the house was a good place to play "hide and seek" so this game quickly became one of our favorites. This was no ordinary hide-and-seek game; it was high powered hide-and-seek. I was usually asked to be the seeker while the two children hid. I could quietly follow their conversations, their plans to trick me, and could track their changes in location and strategy. When I finally presented myself, oh boy, their reaction was precious: they became so excited that they trembled, fell to the floor in uncontrollable spasms of laughter. And they wanted to do it over and over again. I could only speculate that this was their way to work out the pent up stress and emotions of the day...

If parents were successful in forming a positive attachment with the child, by the time the children are three years old or older the family life becomes less stressful and more enjoyable, full of happy moments and activities.

When the children give indications of having settled into the family and they eat well, sleep better, and begin to relate more personally to the parents, I feel that's when we enter the "Golden Years of Adoption."

At this point the family has established patterns, life seems natural and good. It is not so much a daily struggle to adjust, improvise, learn and survive the day.

At one year of age our oldest loved to sit on the kitchen floor banging pots and pans while I prepared meals. He was relaxed and happy. Later on he started to imitate his father who suffered from allergies; he would grab a napkin and while walking behind my husband, he would pretend to sneeze and cough while repeating several times, "Daddy." This was hilarious. It was also an indication of how much the child was relating to his father at such an early age and responding to the environment.

Our second son took a longer period of time to show adjustment. He maintained irregular sleep patterns for a much longer time, had digestive problems well into his second year of life and was, in general a very quiet child as though he did not want to call attention to himself.

The children started to interact with each other, miss each other when apart and help and protect each other. Their distinct personalities began to emerge.

Edward, our younger son, was very independent, always searching for ways to entertain himself. He took everything apart: clocks, toys, telephones. Later on, in elementary school, he would win two first places in Science Fairs with demonstrations and devices created or adapted by him. Later on, in high school, Edward was given the highest recognition granted by the drama department of his school for outstanding performance as stage manager during his junior year. He was, and is, a quiet doer.

Rob, the oldest, was the verbal one; he started to talk before one year of age, and loved repeating difficult words like "ostrich" or "spinach." He would listen to music and children's songs for long periods of time and learn them by heart. At a very early age he demonstrated his affinity towards music, drums being his favorite instrument, an activity he still maintains as an adult. I was told by the director of a Conservatory of Music he attended for three years that Robert was the best drummer she had had at the school. Today, Rob plays several instruments, continues to be an excellent drummer and records music CDs.

As a child, Edward was inquisitive, analytical, and observant. Rob was agile, had good balance and dexterity, and loved physical activities like skating, climbing rocks, walls, and roofs, and hiking and jumping on trampolines. They both loved water activities of all sorts. As adults, Edward became a professional digital designer and Robert pursues his strong interest in music, plays several instruments, records music, while working during the day to earn a living.

Despite knowing nothing about the child's past, or inherited talents and abilities, parents can begin to discover them. This awareness helps in planning activities and programs for the family, and provides a sense of what activities the children would enjoy later in life.

For our family, outings and trips were the highlights of The Golden Years. The visits to Grandma and Grandpa Keane in New York were always a magic adventure, full of surprises and fun. One time, an adventure riding with Grandpa in his sports car, with the top down, standing on the seats and feeling the wind, came to a sudden stop by the police! The ensuing warning ticket has never been forgotten. Trips to the beach, to national parks, to zoos, all provided not just treasured memories, but also topics for many conversations around the dining room table. Although we did not know it at the time, these conversations about our happy times together would provide the foundation for other more difficult conversations later in life. And, of course, their joys were also their parents' joys. Just watching them have fun brought delight into our lives. Memories of these experiences would also soften the stressful times when the children began to understand adoption, the impact of it on their lives as they began to question everything. Providing and enjoying these enriching activities is like putting money in the bank of the family's relationships. They are like a fragile rope to hold on to as the rough waters come, later on.

There are, nevertheless, during these Golden Years, unpleasant situations which arise. Our younger child received a school assignment in second grade, "Draw your family." A simple assignment, right? Our son brought the drawing home to show us, as seen on page 61.

Father, brother, dog, a house in the background and himself, all in stick figures...

I said, "Very good," a typical motherly response.

He said, "The teacher asked me, 'Don't you have a mother? Where is your mother?'"

His answer, "I told the teacher you were in the bathroom."

I said, "What made you say that?"

He then explained, "I did not know which mother the teacher was talking about, if you or my biological mother."

As adoptive parents, we need to understand and accept that our children come to us with emotional wounds. We do not see those wounds but we need to be sensitive enough to be able to interpret and deal with behaviors that might seem to us strange, unfair, and inappropriate. If we keep in mind that our children are psychologically fragile, we can be more sensitive to their needs as they mature.

The question therefore, becomes: How do we understand our children? How do we read the child's behavior? How do we cope with it? Do we think "this child does not like me?" Or do we approach the situation with a "can do" attitude, sensitivity and most importantly, empathy? Because, make no mistake, no matter how much we love our children and demonstrate it, they will constantly test our patience. We are dealing with a child who is grieving but not able to explain it; we are dealing with a child who is feeling unexplained profound loss, pain and sadness and needs a soft shoulder to lean on.

my Family Edward
There's a pool next to the bathroom.
Me
Robert my brother
This is the bathroom.
My mom is in the bathroom.
Daddy
She's washing her hands

In the second grade, Edward drew this picture of his family

Reading books by the pool, top right; having fun in the Andes, center right; early interests, center left.

Loved the water!

Adolescence

Dialogue between an adopted child and his mother:

Mother: "Tell me, dear, what do you wish I had done differently, as your mother, when you were younger?"

Adoptee: "I wish you would have listened to me more."

The subject of adolescence in adoption, as in biological children, deals with deep and complex emotions, states of mind, developmental situations and relationships between children and parents. My addressing of these subjects is not meant to be diagnostic or therapeutic, only informational and exploratory. The book's bibliography offers sources of information for those readers who wish to go deeper into these subjects.

Gregory C. Keck, Ph.D. says in his influential book *Parenting Adopted Adolescents*, "It is a utopia for parents to think that they can control their adolescent children's behavior; the only thing parents can control is themselves."

The words "teen" and "adolescent" can send parents' minds into spins, and even more so when talking about an adopted child. However, adolescents can be wonderful human beings. They are intuitive, sensitive, full of energy and ideas, passionate, and at times, they are unstoppable. They are the not-quite-ripe but almost bursting seeds of a new generation.

During adolescence children are growing in leaps and bounds. Their bones, muscles, brain, mental and language skills are growing, and they are beginning to open themselves towards the world outside the home. They are also becoming aware of their own inclinations, talents, interests, and, most important, their so- much-desired-power of decision making.

As puberty approaches, around 10 or 11 years of age, many things begin to evolve in a teenager's life. But in addition to all the natural biological changes, the adopted teen has to deal with even more complicated issues of identity. Remember the constant wonder in the adoptees mind of "Who am I?"; "Who were my parents?" Dealing with this duality complicates life for both children and parents.

When our children were pre-teens, I came home late at night after an official outing with my husband, and found a note on my pillow:

"Mom, I am leaving home tomorrow morning, I already packed my backpack, I do not want to live here anymore. Love you, Ed."

Coming out of the Golden Years stage my husband and I were still bathed in the glow those years gave us as parents. Adoption was a cinch; the worst was over, we were super parents! We were noticing some changes in behavior like a different taste in music or preferences for clothing styles, new friendships and especially the fact that the children were not as good friends with each other as they had been until then. However, the subtle messages our children's behaviors were giving us went unnoticed by us. So this clear and direct message, "I do not want to live here anymore," shook us. "Why?"; "What's going on?" were among many questions in our minds. Needless to say, I did not sleep at all that night, ready to jump out of bed as soon as I heard the clunk, clunk, clunk of steps coming down the stairs. Fortunately, I did not hear them…Some years later we learned the cause of that statement and of all the background events which provoked it.

Part Three

For all young people, balancing life between the end of childhood and the beginning of early adulthood is challenging and sometimes can lead to despair. The frustrations created by conflicting emotions and feelings can easily rise into higher levels of anger, described by adopted adolescents as "an uncontrolled, unexplainable anger." Other words which can be associated with adolescents are intense, unpredictable, out of control. One day, our child who loved to swim, loved the ocean, snorkeling, anything water, said, "I do not want to go to the pool; I am never going to swim again." What? No amount of questioning and inquiries revealed the reason for this unprecedented decision. A few years later, we learned that the reason had been the existence of a tattoo in our son's upper arm which he was striving to hide.

Adolescence, in general, brings years of turmoil and changes in the lives of biological and adopted teenagers. In conversations with adopting parents when things are not going well, one frequently hears: "What am I doing wrong?" The true answer is we do not intentionally do anything wrong; we are simply unaware of the inner struggles the adopted children are dealing with but are unable to communicate to parents with words. They unconsciously reveal their feelings by means of behaviors which puzzle the adoptive parents and sometimes even the children themselves.

The combination of the possible lagging effects of loss of the birth mother and separation from her, the trauma of early experiences in inappropriate environments, the neurological developments in the adolescent's brain and the hormone changes which happen in the body at this time, are all potential sources of difficulties for effective communication between parents and children, biological or adopted. How things are perceived and interpreted and how adults react to situations, determine the outcome of conflicts within the family and also in the social environment.

In adolescents, the prefrontal cortex which regulates emotions, reasoning and the anticipation of consequences is not fully formed. Adolescent are at the mercy of what neurologists call "the lower brain", or the sub-cortical brain, without the filtering controls of the cognitive, reasoning brain (Daniel Siegel, 2014).The belief now is that the frontal, reasoning lobes do not completely develop until the beginning of the early twenties and even later.

During these developmental years, the teen begins to form attachments outside the family, to give special attention to communicating, not with the parents, but with friends in school or in the neighborhood. They begin to resist common family activities like traveling, having a cookout or watching a movie. Communications can easily come to a standstill during these years.

All parents have an important task: to help their children develop good self-esteem and a healthy self-identity. This task is of the highest importance when the child has been adopted. Let's remember adopted children do not have referents of their own: no family traditions, no known relatives, and no points of identity. "He will be like his uncle John" parents might say about a birth child, or "She will be an accomplished pianist like my sister." All these expectations are based on genetic influences or family traditions. This is where the adoptees are lacking. Today, with open adoptions being more acceptable, adopting parents have more sources of information to incorporate into their repertoire to help the children begin to develop a self-identity, either with their adoptive parents or some other known biological relative the child knows and admires.

Shared moments with Mom, Edward and Robert

With pets Pulga and Shadow in McLean, Virginia

With Grandpa and Grandma in Florida

In Guatemala with tia Amparo, cousin Ines and tio Jorge

Empathic Parenting

To UNDERSTAND THE behaviors of adopted children we must know, remember and accept where they are coming from. If we know the children's past and the effect that past had on them we can begin to feel empathy for their pain and suffering. Feeling empathy is a facilitator for recognizing the needs of other people and makes validation of the person's situation possible. Adoptees yearn for validation of their situation more than any other factor in their lives.

Part of a testimonial from our son Robert,

"For a long time I never thought adoption was an issue within my identity …in life. As far as I was concerned my parents were John and Graciela Keane. Sure, we didn't share any similar physical attributes, but that didn't seem to be an issue, a conflict, a root cause of suffering. The most bothersome thing was when people would ask if I miss my parents, my "real" parents. I would always respond THEY ARE my REAL PARENTS!" I thought I never missed my biological mom and dad…Or so I thought.

And in this declaration lies the real difference between biological and adoptive children and the influence it has in the family dynamics.

Another situation faced by adoptive parents but not by biological parents *is the natural and profound desire adoptees have to know where they came from,* the origin of their biological families, and, very frequently, curiosity about having birth siblings. As early as seems feasible, inform the adopted child of the special circumstances of how he/she came to be yours, but avoid expressing expectations that the child be "special" to make you "proud" because of the way he/she became your child. Adopted children yearn to be loved, to belong. They do not want to be "special." If the child does not see herself as special, being told that she is special causes an extra burden in her life.

Another feeling present in adoptees but not necessarily in biological children, unless they live in an environment of domestic violence, *is the fear of rejection*. The fear of rejection is so influential adoptees usually refuse to ask for favors. Often a simple "no" or slightly critical comment is seen as a rejection. This apparently is one of the reasons why many adoptees declare not to be interested in looking for their biological parents or family. They fear being rejected again.

Guilt and shame are also common because many adopted children express to therapists that they believe they are responsible for what happened to them. They believe that they must have done something very wrong to have been rejected by their birth mother. They will spend their lives either proving that they are indeed "bad," or trying to contradict the feeling of badness they have, by being submissive, by almost disappearing in the background.

One more feeling expressed by adoptees is the *powerlessness over circumstances* they perceive as a permanent condition in their life, even going back to when they were born. All children start their life vulnerable and at the mercy of the adults. As they grow and begin to feel the love and support of parents, of the family members, they begin to develop a sense of belonging and with it a sense of self confidence.

Given their unknown origins, most adoptees have a

need for a clear identity, an identity that distinguishes them from a family where they feel they do not belong. This causes adoptees to ask themselves: "Who am I?"; "Where do I fit?" "How do I know what is expected of me?"

On the face of all these psychological needs and confusions, adopting parents need to walk a tight-rope between being understanding and supportive but not being too permissive because they do not want the child to feel rejected. They need to emphasize the child's skills, talents, and preferences, and pay special attention to referents of the present not of the past. In the case of male adoptees, the adoptive father is especially important as a role model; frequently, an adopted child has some information about the birth mother but usually not about the biological father.

As children approach adolescence they begin to understand reproduction and motherhood, and begin to notice how society highlights the love a mother has for her children, the importance of being a mother, how a mother is willing to risk her life for a child, etc. The adopted teenager wonders: "Why did my mother give me away? Was there something wrong with me? Was it my fault?" These are heavy mental burdens for a young person to bear and are well worth of our empathy.

When our children were about 7 and 5 years of age we decided to take them back to their place of birth. The first morning we were getting ready to go out to visit the city of Buenos Aires, when our oldest said: "I am not going anywhere." We were surprised, and asked him to tell us why not. At first he would just repeat, over and over again, "I am not going anywhere." Finally, he stood in the middle of the hotel room, put his hands on his waist and looking at us, said, "Well, how would you like it if I am walking down the street and this lady I do not know comes straight at me, grabs my hand, and says, 'This is my son; I am taking him back,' and takes me away?"

Our sightseeing plans were obviously delayed while we sat down to hear him and tried to calm his fears. He and I held hands the entire day when out in the street because we reassured him that no lady whatsoever was going to take him away from us!

Many behaviors of adoptees are also a product of their ambivalent feelings about their dual parents: biological and adoptive. For some adoptees the image of the birth mother can be a constant in their minds. Others declared not to care much about her, or think of her only occasionally.

One of our sons recently said, recalling his early years: "I always had a fear of abandonment, of being left alone." He added: "I remember one time after school in 2nd grade all the parents would meet up with the kids after school by the entrance…usually a chaotic mess. At some point between inside and outside of the school I got separated from my mother and instantaneously I felt a sinking feeling of despair and gloom in the pit of my stomach. Confusion dizzied me as I spun in every which way frantically seeking my mother… My pulse quickened and I started tearing up, about to cry, "MOM!"

"Here I am, dear," she calmly said.

"This is an example of how quickly I could go from feeling secure to total desperation." This event was shared by Rob, relating something that happened when he was seven years old.

PART FOUR

Mobile Families

"**M**OM, ARE WE there yet?" Probably all readers have heard this question at one time or another. The fact is in the life of Foreign Service and other mobile families, *there* is rarely predictable or permanent.

A mobile family refers to family groups that, because of work assignments, or by choice, live in a foreign country for fairly extended periods of time. For the purpose of this book, mobile families include missionaries and other religion-based professionals, international business companies' employees, the members of the armed forces, diplomats and other foreign affairs or aid agencies personnel, teachers, graduate students, faculty and research staff, expats at foreign universities or governmental institutions, among others. The field of adoptions involving mobile families is extensive.

For the purpose of this book I will address three demographic groups:

- Parents of any nationality adopting while living in a foreign country

- Foreign parents living in the United States adopting U.S.-born children

- United States-born parents adopting a child from a foreign country and bringing the child to live in the United States. I would like to extend the concept to children who join a family who came from a different culture. All these parents will, by force or by choice, deal with a dominant culture affecting the adopted child's life and a secondary culture that, if respected and maintained, will help the child develop a healthy self-identity.

Closed Adoptions

Families or individuals adopting while living overseas, and sometimes even adopting in the U.S.A., are likely to encounter "closed adoptions." This type of adoption prohibits the adoption agencies, usually a government entity, or a clandestine agency, to give information about the child's origins to adopting parents. These adoptions are very common in many countries for several reasons: a child born out-of-wedlock brings shame to the family involved; or a female baby is not desired due to certain cultural values; or simply because the adoption agency does not want the expense of researching and passing on information to the adopting parents. In many cases, it is the family relinquishing the child who is not interested in establishing or furthering contact with the adoptive family. They do not want to reveal the name of the family or do not have the financial means to maintain a future relationship. I also need to mention adoptions conducted through black markets, when children are either stolen or sold by the birth parents under illegal operations. Sadly, these adoptions are still conducted. All these circumstances make closed adoptions more convenient for the family giving up the child and for adoption agencies. However, they are not ideal for the receiving parents or for the adoptees.

A closed adoption situation will almost certainly bring complications, especially in the area of the relationship between adoptive parents and the child, health issues, inheritance and cultural identification. The more information the adopting family receives, the easier it will be for them to establish a good relationship and bonding with the child, to try to introduce the child's birth culture into their lives as well as to being able to answer questions when the time arrives for the child to want to know where s/he comes from, usually at the onset of adolescence. Many parents prefer or need to travel to the child's country of origin when receiving the child. This gives them an opportunity to get first-hand information about the values, traditions, art and other aspect of the child's country of origin which will facilitate the passing of information to the adoptee later on in life.

However, in many adoption situations, closed adoptions are the only option and, therefore, the receiving families ignore all the negatives and proceed to request and welcome a child granted through a closed adoption.

It is likely that at some point the adoptee will become curious about his/her birth parents and the circumstances of his or her birth. This does not happen in all adoption situations. If and when the situation arises, the adoptive parents should not feel threatened by it, but rather need to offer their support as much as possible. The event of telling the adoptee about his/her background is best to be pursued gradually, perhaps making an agreement that it would better to delay actions until the adoptee is an adult or at least mature enough to absorb bad news (and there probably will be some) as well as good. Also, for closed adoptions, parents need to prepare the adoptee for a possibly long and frustrating search for the biological family which could end with no real information. A good start is to seek out non-identifying information from the adoption agency or state record office regarding any information available about possible genetically related illnesses or other details the birth mother may have provided.

During my conversations with adopting mothers, one of them mentioned that when she went to receive two babies in a foreign country the orphanage had over one hundred young children in its care. In these circumstances it is wishful thinking to expect a complete folder with information about a child being made available for adoption. On the other hand, not everyone feels comfortable establishing an open, on-going relationship with a birth mother. As with everything else, there are exceptions. I have known of cases of open adoptions when the adopting parents, the child and the birth mother established lifelong links to everyone's comfort and advantage.

Closed adoptions are a reality; they will bring future complications but we need to embrace them and the inconveniences they create.

Open Adoptions

Open adoptions are potentially a better choice if we consider issues in the fields of health, medical history or identity. The more information the adopting family receives the easier it will be to try to weave the child's birth culture into the family lives. It facilitates respecting a child's choice of cultural preferences while growing up. It also facilitates being able to answer questions when the time arrives for the child to want to know where s/he comes from, usually at the onset of adolescence.

All these considerations are even more relevant when the adopted child does not physically resemble the adoptive parents. As the child grows, if the family tries to hide the fact that the child is adopted or the adoption circumstances, or if the family diminishes the child's background and culture, difficulties will interfere with the bonding and attachment process and the healthy development of the child. Parents who try to maintain secrets, cover lies with lies, or control rumors around the neighborhood, create dramatic situations. Many adopted persons will eventually desire to know details about the birth family or the adoption and will research, as has been said by adoptees when participating in surveys, interviews and in written testimonials. It is also very likely that at some point in the adoptee's life someone would, willingly or accidentally, pass on the information that the person in question was adopted. When this happens, it comes as a shock to the adoptee and starts a process of mistrust between the adoptive parents and their child.

Are you my mother?

Some of you may know or remember this book. A little bird falls off the nest while attempting to learn to fly; it wanders around trying to find out where it is, what happened to the nest, and, most important, where is its mother? The baby bird wanders around and around asking every creature it encounters, "Are you my mother?" This book was one of my children's favorites in their early years. We read it many times and it elicited several interesting conversations.

When you think about it, an adopted child is in a similar situation as the little bird, always wondering "Who am I, really?"; "How did I end up here?"; "Why was I chosen among many other children?" One adoptee gave the last question a twist when, with a wink and a smile, said: "I guess because I was a cute baby." What a wonderful demonstration of self-confidence!

For Foreign Service families and other mobile families adopting a child of a different race has many implications. I hope your circumstances, reader, are simpler that our family's circumstances. My parents were Colombian but of European ancestors; my husband's parents were Austrian and Dutch; my husband is first generation American born and raised; I am Colombian and our children were born in Argentina and we lived in 8 different countries while our children were growing up. Talk about the need to choose a culture…! We, the parents, already had our preferences and exposing the children to the American and South American cultures allowed them to make choices of their own, enriched at every country we lived in. As someone said, we were nothing less than a "United Nations" family group.

Part Four

For a mobile family the high school years are critical years. We read about it, heard people tell us "no matter what you do, do not move during the last two years of high school" and, of course, we thought they were exaggerating but later discovered the reasons for this advice. It is indeed exhausting and difficult for an adopted teenager to move during those years. They can become unapproachable, deeply sad, and resentful. The parents have a major role in helping the adolescent child accept the new changes and be willing to participate in the adjustments to the new life. If all of this is not perceived or understood by all those involved, the situation can easily deteriorate. During this time, one of our children simply stopped talking to us for a year! This was proof he was in a crisis situation, which was obvious to us; but, not so obvious was how to deal with the situation. Given his prolonged silence for one year we realized we had clearly missed the mark.

Our second son decided to go off to college while we were living overseas. I strongly felt this huge separation from the family was not going to be good for him as indeed it was not. It took several years, still on-going, to repair the damage done during that separation.

I would like to take the liberty to suggest to mobile family adoptive parents a better situation to enter college, especially when the family is assigned overseas, is to have the child start at a community college level or a university in the country of residence, to then transfer later to another institution when the child has adapted to a different life style and has become more independent. Some families I know made arrangements for the child in question to go and live

Drawing by Robert Keane, age 4, to illustrate *Are You My Mother?*

with a relative. Anything would be better than sending him or her off to an entirely new and disconnected situation, like a college campus, away from all support systems.

In our experience, colleges do not provide the close follow-up on freshman students which adopted children of mobile families need. They grow up in very close-knit family groups and communities, where everybody knows everyone else. The sudden rupture of that protective environment can be devastating.

In addition to the emotional and psychological situations there are also practical aspects to be considered. An adoptee needs to know about being adopted when filling out medical questionnaires during a visit to a doctor's office. Writing in "unknown" to questions such as "age of parental death" or "cause of death," among many other questions, is not only unhelpful to a doctor who is trying to learn about a person's medical history, but it also elicits negative, sad feelings in the respondent. As expressed by an adoptee during a survey regarding her feelings about adoption, the person said: "Adoption creates feelings of isolation; it is like a different kind of loneliness." These situations, in themselves, are a good reason to promote and support ancestry research such as provided by 23 & me or Ancestry.com.

The unfairness of being denied potentially critical personal information is also frustrating since the adoptee will also want to tell the children or grandchildren if there are certain illnesses that occur in the birth family such as Parkinson's disease, epilepsies, mental health conditions, developmental delays, etc. A good example of the need to convey to a child the facts about adoption is the case of vaccines given at birth in some countries. Our children were born in Argentina, a country which tests all newborns for tuberculosis. This procedure makes it necessary to avoid giving the child future tests for tuberculosis, tests which are sometimes required to enroll in schools. This makes it mandatory for mobile families to keep detailed medical records regarding not only vaccinations but also other treatments, illnesses treated, surgeries, and any information regarding health problems unique to a country, and to carry those records by hand every time the family moves.

International adoptions bring many opportunities for enriching the family life. If we approach the situation with a little bit of planning, creativity and commitment, these opportunities and new circumstances will eventually become part of the family's life style.

Stress and the Mobile Family

Stress takes a high toll in the lives of families whose members need to adjust to the constant comings, goings and re-adaptations. Having traveled and lived as a Foreign Service family for 37 years I know the family goes into "crisis mode" every time a new change in living conditions happens. The loss of friends, schools, neighborhoods, extended family and support services causes many inconveniences, most of them rather costly emotionally and financially. It is particularly hard on the children. To minimize the effects of the losses and separations, members of the families become sort of "pack rats"—nothing is willingly left behind or abandoned. Moving company workers are surprised by the "stuff" they find in boxes when they unpack at the families' new location; no, not shrunken heads, but empty candy wrappers, or empty soda cans, shoe boxes, broken objects, and the occasional dead insect. These "souvenirs" show that any item that brings back "the familiar left behind and badly missed" becomes special. Not to mention the home itself, girlfriends, pets, school, favorite teachers, etc.

On arriving at a new post, parents need to immediately start looking for the nearest doctor or clinic, school, recreation sites, biking trails, churches. They need to find out if there is someone at this new place the family had befriended at a previous location. The first months of the life of a mobile family are busy, stressful and lonely. Fortunately, today, many corporations, institutions and organizations have established personnel within their ranks who contact and assist new arriving families to give them a hand and deliver orientation packages containing most of the information the family will require to get settled. Also, social media is of immense help in staying in touch with friends and loved ones left behind. Although no doubt helpful, the assistance provided does not eliminate the effect of the losses suffered with each move and the stress the new situation creates.

What is stress?

According to several sources, stress is a natural reaction of the body and mind to any change, physical, environmental or psychological, or a combination of all. If the change requires adjustments, the level of stress depends on the intensity, complexity or frequency of the change. A stressful situation activates biological, anatomical and psychological responses. The individual will may attempt to escape, if the situation is dangerous enough, ignore the situation, or try to cope with it introducing changes in its behavior or environment. When the person feels that s/he cannot cope with the demands of change nor ignore the situation, s/he feels "stressed out," "stressful," or in panic. The name for stress as it is commonly used today was first used around 1936 as a "non-specific response of body and mind to a change or new situation."

Children are particularly affected by stress, and more so adopted children. After each move, they find themselves in a "new vacuum," with all the fragile links they had managed to establish at the previous place, broken. It's back-to-square-one each time. Back to re-asserting themselves, to explain why they look different from their parents, why they speak the parents' language with a different accent. And, if very young, back to creating responses to a new environment.

The "inner teacher" is working full time figuring out what responses are needed in the new situation. Once again, they are disconnected, without referents. The newborn or very young have a double task in their hands: re-adjusting the messages of the "inner teacher" to the new situation while at the same time continuing to grow and develop skills. The memory bank created during the nine months of pregnancy is all but useless and the child needs to start a new memory bank which will help him adjust to the new environment. All of this takes time and energy. The child might sleep too much, or be irritable or develop problems with feeding and sleep habits. As put by an adoptee, "that mysterious psychological link that exists between a birth mother and a baby is broken." And, once again, every time the family moves, the invisible links the adopted child has been busy creating are also broken.

In view of all these given and sometimes unavoidable conditions, what can we do?

You can probably come up with many ideas which would help you and your family cope with these multiple variations in your lives and to help young children feel and experience a new place in a positive way. Accommodations such as keeping familiar objects, smells, sounds, foods; pets also help. Transporting a pet to a new location, city or country, is complex and costly but it is probably the # 1 action which would help the children begin to feel some normality in their lives.

Connecting with previous friends or acquaintances; establishing new friendships at the new place also help and can be done by means of sport activities, clubs, joining classes such as art, language, history of the city. The parents need to join associations which organize activities where the new arrivals will feel on familiar ground, such as picnics, bake sales, theater groups, hiking clubs, boys' and girls' scouts, dancing classes, language classes, community libraries; if affordable, joining a social club with sports facilities is also great to make new friends.

A favorite activity for families with young children in various places where we lived was joining a play-group; the friendships made at play groups can last a lifetime.

When in a new place do not wait to be invited to homes, do the inviting yourself. Opening your home for community or school activities or events is always a good opportunity to begin friendships.

Today, modern technology offers great opportunities to stay in touch at a distance using the many social media systems. An excellent idea is keeping a blog to share your life with the family left behind; using Skype, Zooming and What's App, help in sharing the new foods you have tried, the classes you are taking and how fluent you are in the new country's language.

Conclusions

B Y NOW, READERS, perhaps you are thinking, "Well, who wants to adopt, then?" I do not intend to discourage or scare those who are considering adopting. Adopting is a beautiful, heartwarming experience that will enrich your life and will change you into a different person. But I want potential parents to walk into the situation, not blindfolded like we did, but with the eyes wide open, and carrying a bag full of skills and responses which will make your parenting task easier.

Adoption is not for the weak of heart nor is it the solution for a failing marriage, therapy for mental health problems or a way to be accepted socially. It is a life- changing experience with immense rewards for all those involved as long as we understand its challenges and are prepared to deal with them.

Knowing what the children have experienced before they joined their adoptive families will help parents understand many of the adoptee's attitudes and behaviors. As I have shown throughout the book, not all adopted children behave in the same way nor react to adoption the same as others. Nevertheless, the more one reads testimonials and books about adoption, the more one realizes that there is a clear trend, a commonality of feelings and behaviors revealed by adoptees that have had the courage to open up and talk about their experiences.

The more we understand the child, try to acknowledge the pain and try to implement ways of establishing a strong relationship, and better communication, beginning with the years of attachment and bonding, the more we will be able to facilitate the process of grieving and healing, of coming to terms with his or her life and special circumstances.

In adoption, the process of becoming united as a family involves, first, *understanding* of the situation; second, *love* for the child we are raising as our own; and, third, *engagement*, in a positive, pro-active approach to parenting, beyond what would be considered "enough." There is no "enough" in adoptive parenting…

Parenting, in adoption, brings rewards and challenges, just like in a biological family. And the ultimate reward is to launch our children, as adults, into their own lives, with their own family and fulfilled dreams. This is the gold star in adoption. We all need to aim at reaching for that star for our sake and the sake of those who need us.

As expressed by an adoptee:

"Adoptive parents need to be very proud of themselves for having taken the chance and the responsibility of raising someone else's child in the best way they can. This would sustain them during the inevitable squabbles and difficulties that occur between any parent and child. Only patience and love can overcome the inevitable pain, or at least confusion, the adoptee will feel when he/she realizes that they were given up by their birth parents. And hopefully they will come to learn enough of the truth that they would realize that they were far better off being raised by their adoptive parents."

There are many children who need parents, need a home and a supportive environment. An adoptive mother, a friend of mine, said to me she had decided not to celebrate Adoption Month (November). She clearly had conflicting feelings. She said, "Our journey has been hard…but it also gave us (meaning she and her husband), and the children, a family which we all wanted."

Understanding and accepting that the child we love and treasure, protect when sick, but who is a bundle of confusion and contradictions and can even be offensive towards us, is not an easy task. It can create currents of stress in relationships, antagonisms, and even sheer desperation. Each one of these behaviors and many others require that we, the parents or caregivers, adjust our responses and corresponding behaviors to meet the child's needs even if those behaviors are difficult to understand.

I would like to close with the words of an adoptee to whom I have granted the Gold Star of success because of the results of his adoption. Despite a difficult family situation as he grew up and due, almost entirely, to his grit and positive attitude, he managed to make a success of his life. He said, talking as an adoptee to adoptive parents:

"Always assure your son or daughter that you consider them as important to you and love them as much (but not more) as if they were your birth child."

Because that is what they are, *our sons and daughters,* not our adopted sons or daughters. And we do, at the end, love them as such.

ADOPTEES TALK: TESTIMONIALS

Testimonial One

FOR A LONG time I never thought adoption was an issue within my identity as an individual in life. As far as I was concerned my parents were John and Graciela Keane. Sure, we didn't share any similar physical attributes but it didn't seem to be an issue, a conflict, a root cause of any suffering or dilemma in my life. The most bothersome thing was when people would ask if I missed my parents. My "REAL" parents. I would always respond, "THEY ARE my REAL parents!" And I thought I never missed my biological mom and dad. Truth be told I learned to cope pretty much from a young age with the fact that I would probably never get to know my biological parents. It didn't bother me. It didn't affect me. Or so I thought.

Now looking back, I see that it actually did have some lasting effects on me subconsciously. I don't think I started coming to this conclusion until maybe about 5 years ago. Facilitating this realization were my spiritual studies and other things that were occurring in my life. So, when my mother's book was mentioned it actually coincided with some of my own spiritual development. I had on my own come to conclude that I had abandonment and rejection issues on a deeper level. Unresolved grief transformed into anger towards certain outlets. It was more of a deep feeling of not fitting in, internally. In this life I had certain repeated fears and obsessions and ego trips that I couldn't let go of until I realized that I DID fear being left alone in this world. But I also knew that along with these feelings I recognized was the power to overcome them, so I did. I worked at it and little by little, I have come to a better place now. I did have to go to a multitude of "shrinks" while growing up partially because my parents and I lacked the ability to communicate as a family unit or as understanding, compassionate human beings.

As a child, I did feel the separation of what most would call a "normal" life. Despite what people think about their proper families I always felt they were lucky to know where they came from at least in the superficial sense. What I didn't realize is that this would be the beginning of a seemingly long line of division between my parents and me. Later, separation progressed as the apparent differences on the surface between us took a turn for the worst and started causing more and more tension in me, becoming hurtful, verbal disagreements and reasons to lash out. A rebellious nature blossomed in part due to this. From a frustrated space in which I felt no one understood me. Sounds like a redundant teen cliché but I now realize that what at first seemed to be a romantic estrangement from my biological parents slowly twisted into an alienation from my entire close family. One, because I didn't share their outlook on life, religion, politics, humor, music and so on. And two, simply because we didn't share the same look at all on the outside.

Related to some earlier issues, I had a fear of abandonment, a fear of being left alone. I remember one time after school in 2nd grade all the parents would meet up with the kids after school by the entrance for pick-up and it usually was a chaotic mess. At some point between the inside and outside of the school I got separated from my mother and instantaneously I felt a sinking feeling of despair and gloom in the pit of my stomach. Confusion dizzied me as I spun in every which way frantically seeking my mother out with my eyes skyward. My pulse quickened and I started tearing out "MOM!"

"Here I am, Dear," she calmly said.

Just an example of how quickly I could go from feeling secure to total desperation. Another quick example is how I would never want to be separated from my mother even while going to the bathroom. I would ask her to stand by the stall door so I could see her feet. I really was terrified of being abandoned. At school, an amusement park or the zoo. It didn't matter. There are more examples but I digress.

I went from a form of slight autophobia to a feeling of full isolation but not in the external sense, more on a subjective level. I always have managed myself well in social situations due in part to my father's job. I always had to adapt myself to new social situations. I looked calm on the surface, yet I always have been an anxious person beneath and now I know that this is in part due to the life changing event of being separated from my mother and father along with other things that were occurring in my life. My fears of being abandoned manifested in my feeling as if I HAD been abandoned by everyone all around me. I didn't take rejection well if it came from someone I truly cared for. In the end however, no one or nothing has made me feel more secure, more loved and worthy than my adopted parents. Yes, truly more than my biological parents ever could and did. Perhaps that is the tragic irony of the maladjusted adoptee. The validation we seek outside and emptiness we feel inside are conflicts that require much introspection and work not merely solved by slipping into the societal mold of what a healthy family should look and/or act like. Through inner growth and life experiences I have managed to come to understand things more. It wasn't until I was in my 30's however, that I came to accept the notion that adoption actually did play a role in the estrangement I had felt throughout my life in general. I do not BLAME adoption or being adopted or my biological parents or any of that. Not at all. But as with any crucial circumstance that changes the trajectory of a person's life, being adopted affected me no matter what I would have liked to have thought about it. Little things that added up. For me it was specifically those things mentioned before and then some others: the superficial judgments about my being based on the cultural merit of adoption. I was pitied a lot. That is no one's fault, it just arises out of compassion really. But it made me feel as if there was something wrong with me on a subconscious level. Or it made me feel less worthy. I now take my differences and wear them proudly on my sleeve. It took some time to connect the dots between the things I was feeling inside and some reoccurring themes in my life, but I now see some things more clearly.

With a rocky start to adolescence I used it as fuel to drive my art. But lacking a solid spiritual upbringing as well, I did begin to tumble here and there. I will mention here that constantly being uprooted from my environment every 3 years or so in stressful ways added to some confusion in my life but that is just what came with my father's job -- I do not see it as a hardship. It was a blessing in countless ways to have been brought up internationally. It paved the way for the spiritual steps I was to find at 22. The hardest part for me however was when at 16 I was forced to go to a boarding school for the remaining 2 years of high school. The supposed best years of high school were more like my worst and were also the beginning of a volatile spiral in my life. Academically I was on the Headmasters List with a 3.4-3.7 G.P.A. so that never suffered as much as my internal states did. In fact, I used the boredom of the boarding school to maintain my grades. However, in relationships I also developed a fear of being left. And if I was left it made it all that much worse. I now realize I had developed a fear of abandonment that stemmed back to high school, back to elementary, back to my first days of being alive. Yet, the Love I needed to cultivate was within me as well as without me. Now I am happy to say that my parents and I have mended the gap between us and have a very loving and respectful relationship. In conjunction with the things I have come to realize as I live on came the opportunity to share my own personal revelations with the adoption world.

My only real suggestions as to what a parent can do help support their adoptive child is to be there to support the entire being of the child even the sides that don't make sense. My parents did the best they could but they themselves lacked a spiritual upbringing. I craved one. It wasn't enough to do things "just because". At least be patient with one another and strive to move closer without judgments and grudges. Don't try to over-analyze things but listen with an open mind and heart. If a child doesn't follow the path a parent desires then more communication is needed perhaps, not forcible demands or ultimatums.

For any adoptees, I pray you seek out truthful answers to your deepest questions. There are some things your adoptive parents cannot help you with, you must find the answers out for yourself. I feel adoption is a special kind of life to be born into. One that requires you to absorb the love from life itself and then cultivate a love of your own within yourself and then outwards on. Almost as if to say, yes, we couldn't count on anyone else for support the moments after birth yet, DO reach out and spread the love that we can once we find it. I feel most adoptees may struggle with this question of identity and belonging at some point within their lives more powerfully than others may, given that the question of "who am I" is constantly staring us in the face from childhood all the way up to our adult lives. It is a life started out with question and bewilderment. But one can make sense of it with careful introspection and care towards oneself and one's new adopted family. And perhaps don't ever forget that the circumstances of life that brought you all together were unique and while on one hand it may be a kind of family situation that takes a lot of effort to develop and uphold, it is also the kind of family that doesn't discriminate and actually strives to create a more unified, wholehearted world.

Testimonial 2

In responding to the following statement, "Contrast the feeling of the happy adoptive parents welcoming their *much desired child* and the state of internal turmoil in the child," an adoptee commented, "I heard this so much from my parents, how much they wanted to have me and my brother. By telling us this I understand they wanted to make up for the rejection of having been given up and I know they must have been very disappointed not to have been able to have their own children. I am sure they were also very grateful they were able to adopt us. But how healthy is it to be wanted versus valued, desired versus wanted, protected versus taught? I grew up more like an object that was here only to serve than a human being with her own rights…

Everyone has so-called flaws but not everyone sees them as something to be ashamed of. Finding those people is my blessing. Working through the shame and separating myself from the judgment of others is on-going. Learning to identify who I want to be is my choice and no one has a say in that; it has taken a lifetime."

Testimonial 3

"THE STORY I was told was that a favorite cousin when I was bragging about my daddy said, "He is not your Daddy," which probably upset me greatly until my parents explained what adoption was and how they came to have me. This made it okay I guess because I grew up comfortable with it. Good thing because when I was a senior in high school I applied to the Air Force Academy and they required a copy of my adoption papers which I read for the first time. The word illegitimate was mentioned a couple of times plus a statement that the father had not been identified and my birth mother had relinquished all rights to me. As you can imagine this was a shocking to read, even though I had known already because it brought harsh reality to an abstract concept.

I don't remember my adoptive parents being upset or angry but instead were hurt and disappointed that I should want to find out about my birth parents after all they had done for me. They just did not understand."

Unsolicited Advice

HELPFUL BEHAVIORS AND attitudes which facilitate the relationship with an adopted child

After 38 years along the adoption road I will not tell you that it has been easy, but I will say it is worthwhile. We owe the richness of our life today to our adult children and we value their presence in our lives, despite the difficult times and obstacles we have all navigated.

Here are some thoughts about specific parental behaviors, attitudes and values our family found useful in maintaining positive and loving relationships.

1. **Birthdays can be difficult for adoptees**. Celebrate them only if child wants a celebration and shows enthusiasm. If child seems bothered or unhappy celebrate another occasion such as the day the adoption became final, the day child joined the family. Or, as one of our sons once suggested, "Let's celebrate a non-birthday!"

2. **Pay attention to the adoptee's choice** of movies, television programs, books, or events. Many times they provide an opening for conversations about adoption.

3. **Share with your child all the information you have** about their origins, places, dates of adoption, no matter how small it might seem. Keep a log of events and be consistent when they ask questions and you tell them the story; every detail is important to the

child. One of our children once said to us, when I was recounting the narrative of their adoption, "that is not how it happened," because I had slightly changed a small detail of the story.

4. **React slowly when confronted with a new, unexpected situation.** Observe, absorb and connect the dots before taking action. Remember adoptees have a part of themselves they dearly protect from others; they might give clues about how they feel but might not be open and direct about it.

5. **Give frequent signs of approval and encouragement.** As long as safety and social rules allow it, it is best to err on the side of being enthusiastic rather than demanding perfection.

6. **Respect your child's preferences.** Your adoptive child has a different gene pool and cultural background. Do not expect him or her to always agree with you or your family values.

7. **Acknowledge the pain, reality and impact of adoption** when the appropriate moment presents itself. According to testimonials by adoptees, they are constantly aware of being adopted, in all circumstances. For example, another child at the playground may say, "that woman is not your mother; you do not look like her," or the adoptee might overhear comments about adoption between two teachers or neighbors. When an adoptee goes to see a doctor they have to fill out questionnaires; common questions include: "At what age or what

year did your parents die?" These are reminders of what they lost, and how much they lost.

8. **Be cautious with potentially harmful comments.** Common remarks like "you are a naughty boy" or "I do not like it when you do that" as well as the "or else" threats are taken hard by adoptees as signs of rejection.

9. **Avoid unnecessary separations** that could be perceived by the adoptee as a sort of abandonment. Events like a summer program away from home, attendance to a boarding school, sending the child alone to spend time with relatives hardly known, if not desired by the child, leave an imprint.

10. **Be aware of behavioral red flags.** The separation from the birth mother left a wound which some researchers believe affects the child for many years or life. Unresolved grief is many times the cause of undesirable behaviors and behaviors that "push the limits" are a common manifestation of defiance provoked by fear and anxiety. "Unspoken grief is unresolved grief." (anonymous saying)

11. **Remember**: adoption is not a bad word. Do not justify and explain adoption at every step of your child's life. Do not highlight your child as adopted if you have biological children.

12. **Err on the side of trust** instead of questioning and doubting when first presented with a difficult situation.

13. **Use eye contact when talking with your child.** Eye contact puts you more closely with your child's inner self.

14. **Facilitate close physical proximity.** Hand holding, sitting close to each other, walking together and hugging are all good ways to avoid emotional distancing.

15. **Try to be generous, loving and accepting.** Raising and adoptive child is not about the parents but rather about the child. Adoptive parents are, often, the only life-line that adoptee has in life.

16. **Accept and support your child's desire to learn about his/her origins.** Try to obtain information about the biological family, country of origin, its culture and traditions; help the child research if there is interest. Do not feel threaten by this natural need. Many times adoptees want to learn about their biological origins but do not want to meet the relatives, and have no intention of leaving the adoptive parents.

Glossary

Adoptee – person who was adopted

Attachment – love, fondness, maternal love, affection, sympathy

> **Positive:** good feelings, approval

> **Negative:** bad feelings, rejection, antagonism

Biological children – a child conceived rather than adopted by a specified parent, and therefore carrying genes from the parent. (https://www.dictionary.com/browse/biological-child)

Bonding – connection, interconnection, regard, affection, bond of union or belonging

Closed adoptions – adoption process which keeps secret records, unrevealed information, and denies the adoptee a right to records of the adoption history

Embryo, fetus – unborn child

Empathy – a vision or thought attached to feelings for another person or for a cause, fancy, a thought of acceptance and understanding towards someone else's suffering

Endometriosis – medical condition that occurs when the tissue that lines the uterus (womb) grows outside it, as in ovaries or fallopian tubes; if untreated, it produces infertility

Engagement – commitment; undertaking efforts to fulfill a promise; to be deeply involved with another person or persons

Genetic – part of a chain of generations; children brought forth through a natural birth

Imprint – retention in the memory; remembered

Mobile Family – family which changes domiciles frequently, from city to city or country to country, due to a career, occupation or assignment

Montessori, method and philosophy – educational approach to teaching young children based on respecting the children's natural abilities and self-motivation

Mosaic – image that combines groups of elements, colors, figures, in an organized or disorganized but agreeable way. Art term also applied to other disciplines

Open Adoptions – adoption process which allows all members involved (adoptee, birth mother and adoptive parents) access to all records and information related to the child's history, adoption legal procedures and identifying elements of all members, places of origin and circumstances

Primal Wound – a concept or idea proposing any child goes through a traumatic experience when separated from the birth mother at birth or soon after.

Psyche – concept which refers to all the elements of the human mind, conscious and unconscious; it could also address the emotions of a person

Puberty – one of the stages in the development of a human being, between the ages of eleven and 16 years

Relinquish – to give up; to cede to others someone or something

Species – mankind; human race

Trust – assurance; faith; confidence

Unconscious – unrecognized; undetected; not aware of

Validate – accept as true, recognize as true; make or declare something legal, factual; confirmation of something

BIBLIOGRAPHY

Ainsworth, Mary, *Attachment and the growth of love, 1912*, YouTube, 2015

Berlingham-Brown, Barbara, *Why didn't she keep me?* Langford Books, South Bend, Indiana, 1994

Bowlby, John, *Baby's pain at loosing birth mother*, 1980

Attachment and Loss, Vol. III, New York: Basic books

Chamberlain, David, *Babies remember birth*, 1988

The Connected Child, Second Edition, McGraw-Hill Education, May, 2020

Dennis, Laura, Editor, *Adoption Therapy, an anthology*, Entourage Publishing, 2014

Dewar, Gwen, Ph. D., *Empathy in Children and Teens: a Guide for the Science Minded*, 2010-2016

Dewar, Gwen, Ph.D., *The Newborn Senses*, CA, 2017-2019

Eldridge, Sherrie, *Twenty Life Transforming Choices Adoptees Need To Make,* Pinon, Colorado, 2003

Eldridge, Sherrie, *Twenty Things Adopted Kids Wish Their Adoptive Parents knew*, Dell Trade Paperback, New York, 1999

Gage, William L., *Readers Guide to Adoption* & related literature, www.wmlgage.com

Goleman, Daniel, *Emotional Intelligence*, Bantam Books, 1997

Granju, K. A., & Kennedy, B. *Attachment and Parenting*. Simon & Schuster, 1999

Grubb, Lynn, *The Adoptee Survival Guides*, ed., 2015

Keck, Gregory C., Ph.D., Kupecky, Regina, LSW, *Parenting Adopted Adolescents*, Revised and updated, NAVPRESS, 2009

Montessori, Maria, M.D., *The Absorbent Mind*, revised and updated, Holt Paperbacks, NY, N.Y., 1995

PBS Documentary, https://www.pbs.org/newshour/show/why-reducing-a-pregnant-womans-toxic-stress-can-improve-the-health-of-her-unborn-child, Dec.19, 2019

Staff, Rachel, *Parenting Adopted Teenagers*, Jessica Kingsley Publishers, London and Philadelphia, 2016

Soll, Joe, *A Path to Recovery*, Amazon.com

Verrier Nancy Newton, *The Primal Wound*, Gateway Press, Inc., Baltimore, MD., 21st edition, 1991

Woolis, Rebecca, MFT, *When Someone You Love Has a Mental Illness*, Penguin Group (USA) Inc., New York, 1992

Zeedyk, Suzanne, *Parent/Infant Relationship*, Dundee, 2014

Zeedyk, Suzanne, *Saber Tooth Tigers and Teddy Bears*, connected baby Ltd; 2 edition (April 14, 2020)

Zinsser, William, *Writing About Your Life*, Marlowe & Company, NY, 2004

OTHER RESOURCES

Adoption Council of Ontario; Family Helper Magazine, Toll free 1-877-adopt-20; info@adoption.on.ca

Center for Adoption Support and Education. General inquires, Phone (301) 476-8525, Northern Virginia, Caseadopt@adoptionsupport.org

https://www.helpguide.org/articles/parenting-family/what-is-secure-attachment-and-bonding.htm

Joint Council on International Children's Services (JCICS), http://jcics.org

Multiple videos and programs, therapy sessions, advice on YouTube:

For example, Kati Morton, therapist, Tuesdays and Fridays

https://www.youtube.com/katimorton/join

National Council for Adoption: www.adoptioncouncil.org

National Organization on Fetal Alcohol Syndrome (NOFAS), www.nofas.org

Center for Adoption Support and Education, www.adoptionsupport.org

Jessica Kinsley Publishers, https://www.jkp.com/adoption

adoptionmagazine.org, articles, Blog, 24/7 services

www.magzter.com, digital subscriptions

Adoptive Family Magazine, https://www.adoptivefamilies.com

Leahy, Meghan, on parenting articles and coaching, chats,

Washingtonpost.com/advice, Questions to: Meghan@mlparentcoach.com

https://www.washingtonpost.com/people/meghan-leahy/

Anonymous responses to set of questions addressed to adoptees posted for two years in a website called "An Adoption Journey"

About the Author

Graciela Congote Keane, a retired Foreign Service spouse, holds a B.A. in Psychology from Indiana University and an M.A. in Early Childhood Special Education from George Washington University. She is a certified Montessori educator and has been a teacher, instructor, counselor, avid reader, artist and gardener. Originally from Colombia, Graciela has lived in the United States and ten other countries, sometimes as a member of the Foreign Service community and at other times as a private citizen. She and her husband, Ambassador John F. Keane, are the parents of two adult sons.

Graciela and John served in the United States Foreign Service/State Department for 37 years. After their last assignment and once back in the USA, Graciela decided to go over all their life experiences and the experiences of their children, both as adoptees and as Foreign Service members, and concluded she needed to write about the lessons learned during those years. It was a therapeutic, slow process that involved the entire family. The non-fiction narrative *Joys and Sorrows of Adoption* is the result of those years of living, reflecting and writing.

Contact:
Graciela Congote Keane
6512 Elmdale Road
Alexandria, VA 22312
Email: gckeane@hotmail.com